Texas Dissident
Dispatches from a Diminished State, 2006-2016

by

E. R. Bills

EAKIN PRESS **Fort Worth, Texas**
www.EakinPress.com

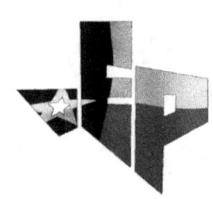
Other Books by E.R. Bills

- *Texas Obscurities: Stories of the Peculiar, Exceptional and Nefarious*
- *The 1910 Slocum Massacre: An Act of Genocide in East Texas*
- *Black Holocaust: The Paris Horror and a Legacy of Texas Terror*

Table of Contents

*This book is dedicated to
Tristan, Rebecca, Kyle and Kevin.*

Acknowledgments

Special Thanks to Gayle Reaves, Kim Peterson, the *Fort Worth Weekly*, the *Fort Worth Star-Telegram* and *Dissident Voice*.

Foreword

Every year for the last decade or so, friends from all over have asked me what I'm still doing in Texas.

I always give the same answer: *It's my home.*

It's also, unfortunately, home to legions of heavily armed, anti-intellectual bigots that occasionally make *The Walking Dead* look like a Macy's Thanksgiving Day Parade.

A war is being waged and Texas comprises one of the trenches. It would be easy to migrate to some Liberal enclave on the East or West Coast, but that would mean giving in. And giving in isn't very Texan.

When I set out to compile these writings, I had no idea how prolific I'd been for the ten-year stretch they cover. I attribute the output to how difficult it was to watch things hit the skids in this state and across the nation during that period. Wholesale devolution, paranoia for profit, paranoia as patriotism, persecution for political gain and crippling ignorance vouchsafed as sacred virtue—a few of us needed to at least pretend to be sane. I'm not sure I was a good candidate for the call, but I put my shoulder to it when I could.

Regardless—at this late date—the damage we've done to our state, our educational system and our political process is considerable and members of the minority sentient population inch forward through the fog of their neighbors' gun lusts, secessionist fantasies and sad, blind conservatism.

If there's a silver lining to this hellishness, it's that it may well have girded us for what we face now. And what we must do.

Keep reading.

E. R. Bills

Deep in the Heart of Bullpucky

When I get moving every day I often grab the newspaper and skim it over breakfast. There's usually not much that helps me wake up, but one December morning a few years back was an exception. On page 7B under the subhead "Redistricting," I took particular notice of a quote from U.S. Representative Michael Burgess, a Republican from Lewisville. Burgess observed that "Anytime you can add Texans to the roster in Congress, it's good for the country." My brow furrowed.

Taken at purely face value, I'm sure most Texans would agree. We are after all Texans, and it plays to our sense of pride and Lone Star swagger.

But flip on just two or three lights in the unused rooms upstairs and it becomes apparent that this claim is long on hat but short on cattle.

Texas is after all home to U.S. Representative Joe Barton. He's the beady-eyed Republican sycophant from Arlington who actually cried and apologized to BP during the Deepwater Horizon oil spill hearings. It wasn't one of our finer moments. In fact, it might be one of the most embarrassing moments in the history of the U.S. Congress.

Texas is also the home state of former U. S. House Majority Leader Tom "The Hammer" DeLay. Most people remember him from the 2009 season of *Dancing with the Stars*. But before he cha-cha-ed to the The Troggs 1966 hit "Wild Thing," he stepped down as House Majority Leader after he was indicted for money laundering (in 2005).

Eventually, DeLay—who was also a K Street lackey who said his proudest moment was intervening to keep Terri Schiavo's feeding tube from being removed (also in 2005), and this after un-plugging his own comatose father following an accident in 1988. And did I mention his right-hand lobbyist was Jack Abramoff?

Texans also have to claim U.S. Senator John Cornyn, as in corn cob in each ear. He's remained steadfastly deaf to any discussions of climate change or global warming and he's never met a polluter he didn't like. He voted against banning drilling in the Arctic National Wildlife Refuge, reducing fossil fuel usage by 40% (instead of 5%), ending subsidies for oil and gas exploration, factoring oil and gas smokestacks in mercury regulations and considering climate change in federal project planning. During Cornyn's long and undistinguished career in the Senate, the League of Conservation Voters has awarded him a score of 0% for his voting record on legislation aimed at protecting the environment. He's an all-around swell guy and visionary.

And then there's Louie "Gomer" Gohmert, the bellwether of batshit. His homegrown loutishness includes: 1) suggesting we shouldn't be wasting our time acknowledging or protecting LGBTQ rights because if human beings are ever forced to flee Earth, same-sex couples would be useless in terms of colonizing the moon; 2) claiming he opposes gun control because same-sex marriages lead to bestiality; and 3) insisting immigrant women are having babies in the United States to create a sleeper army that will one day mobilize and "destroy our way of life."

Oh, and we can't forget Rep. Burgess. In 2013, he claimed he opposed abortion because fetuses masturbate in the womb.

Yep.

(Sorry, mom.)

But seriously.

The headlines don't lie. Texas politicians have been a joke.

It's not as if there's a pattern, here. I mean we're not a state that would let a transplanted Yankee weasel from a Big Oil family seize the governor's office after running a few companies into the ground, serving as part-owner of a pro baseball team and then shooting the state bird. And we certainly wouldn't permit the same cretin to bluff his way into the White House, lie us into a war, turn American soldiers into war criminals or sit idly by while the middle class became an endangered species.

None of that stuff could happen right under our noses, right?

Let me rephrase. *None of that stuff could happen right under our noses after Rick Perry or the time he went on to head the department he famously couldn't remember the name of. Right?*

Right?

Sorry, but there might have been a time when Texas politicians at the national level weren't an embarrassment, but it was at least a half-decade or so before this millennium started. And it doesn't look like there'll be a change in our political delegation any time soon. We have a State Board of Education that thinks the Scopes Monkey Trial was a mouthwash taste-test involving Curious George. We have a state Railroad Commission that's sat on its thumbs so long regarding air quality standards that they're no longer opposable. The thumbs or the Commission. At one point during the Barnett Shale natural gas grab, the EPA was even forced to step in to administer air permits.

And then there's the bizarro flip on the state's most wildly successful marketing campaign, "Don't Mess with Texas." *How is accepting and storing radioactive waste (in Andrews County) from three dozen other states not "messing" with Texas?*

I was born in Texas and I'm as Texan as the next guy, but I've learned to face the facts. If your IQ is over seventy-five and you're not ignorant, misinformed or an employee or beneficiary of the oil and gas industry, expect a tough go of it around here. Most of us aren't just drinking the Red (state) Kool-Aid; we're guzzlin' it from a boot. And the Kool-Aid imbibers seem to outnumber the level heads by a country mile.

We vote against our own interests. We thumb our nose at legislation passed to protect us.

America doesn't need more Texans in Congress. We elect morons, crooks and male chauvinist pigs.

It needs more Texans to wake up and smell the bullpuckey.

No Boundaries

Fort Worth Weekly • *January 13, 2010*

On the morning of December 28, 2009, I woke to a big surprise. My tent and the ground outside it were covered in snow. And it was still coming down.

The day before, I had hiked into the Chisos Mountains of Big Bend National Park. I had hoped to reach the South Rim but, at 7500 feet it got dark on me and I had to camp. I pitched my tent at the elbow of a switchback and, then, to avoid attracting any critters, stuffed my food items into a bag and tossed it up into a tree about fifty-feet from my campsite.

The snow worried me. How much more would there be? Would it make the trails and passes dangerous? I decided to exit the Chisos Basin and head back down. I packed up my tent and retrieved my foodstuff.

The snow on the trail was completely fresh, and I appeared to be the only traveler in the silent Basin wonderland. There was no sign of another living creature for the first half hour of the hike.

I'd forgotten moments like this were possible, especially sitting behind a desk. Taking orders, giving orders. Conforming.

The silence of the trail was like the glass. I saw some of the things I had been missing and the possibilities I'd dismissed and forgotten. There, all around me, in the mountain air and prickly Chisos brush, I felt alive and vital in a way I hadn't in years.

At the trail turnoff for Juniper Canyon, I was reveling in the moment and still amazed that I was alone in nature and part of it. Then I spotted something that broke the spell. There in the fresh snow was an animal track, the foot pad about 3.5 inches in diameter with five small toe prints on top. The impression was fairly

4

fresh and the print was the first of several heading in the same direction as me.

It was a black bear, probably 300- or 400-pounds, and it was somewhere ahead of me. The print was unmistakable, mystical and mind-blowing.

The black bear is endangered in Texas; they had all but disappeared from the Chisos Mountains until bears coming up through Mexico re-established the species. I—we—had encroached on the black bears' habitats for years, practically leaving them no place to live. But, thanks to their Mexican kin, they were back.

I was glad nature knew no borders.

When I settled into a warm motel room that night, I thought about the bear prints and started weaving a clever, satirical piece around the idea of almost stumbling into a furry, 400-pound illegal alien that the federal government was currently welcoming into this country with open arms and spending our tax dollars to support and protect. I thought I would blame the exorbitant cost of our healthcare system on him and complain that, despite the good things one could say about the bears, they were still here illegally and utilizing our social services without paying taxes or learning to speak English. I had decided to use the bear as a humorous vehicle for mocking the ignorance and hypocrisy that clouds our views on immigration.

But I just told the story instead.

Back on the trail, I took a break and let the bear be on his way. I never saw him, but, thankfully, he also never saw me. I was the alien there, and he was the native. I was sure his policy on newcomers was more humane than ours, but I didn't want to push my luck.

He was much better as a bear than as an allegory. And I liked sharing the world with him.

It's an Ugly Time in America

Fort Worth Star-Telegram • *September 20, 2009*

Around my junior or senior year at Aledo High School in the mid-80s, a deceased African-American transient was found tangled up in a barbed wire fence near Interstate 20. Authorities determined that he had wandered out there and died of exposure. A kid in my class saw the body. When describing what it was like, my classmate indicated that it was no big deal because it wasn't like finding a dead man. "It was just a dead nigger."

There was only one African American kid in my class at Aledo. His father was a normal, law-abiding citizen who used to get pulled over by law enforcement personnel about once a month, just because he was black and a black man driving around in our community looked suspicious.

After college and a few years in Austin, I returned to the Fort Worth area and met and married a beautiful African American woman. After our third child was born, we moved to Aledo to be closer to my parents and raise our kids. One day a co-worker who was also a member of the Willow Park Volunteer Fire Department (an adjacent town which feeds into Aledo ISD) received a call on his radio reporting an "NIWP." I asked him what an "NIWP" was. He said it was a "Nigger in Willow Park." I confronted him and informed him my wife was African-American. His facial features shrunk into a disgusted grimace. Commenting on our marital union, he said, "That Ain't Right."

Right or wrong, we stayed in Aledo and I began to think things were changing. Then, Barrack Obama ran for president.

My kids encountered theretofore unheard racial slurs from classmates and were bothered by the petty prejudices the school seemed to tolerate more than discourage. My wife and I were disturbed, but we assumed the unabashed bigotry would subside after the election was over. Unfortunately, it didn't.

A couple of weeks ago, one of my oldest son's high school teachers asked the class what they thought of Obama. Many of my son's classmates said Obama was the Anti-Christ, vaguely alluding to passages from the book of Revelation. I was shocked and wondered which local church fostered such inanity.

Then, last week, one of my son's instructors asked students to record in their journals how they felt about the school refusing to air the live broadcast of Obama's speech on education.

My son usually keeps a low profile, but on this subject he expressed his sense of frustration and alienation. In his journal he wondered if Obama's speech would have been televised if he had been an "old white guy like most presidents." His sentiment cut to core of the issue.

If George Bush or John McCain were president and either wished to address American classrooms on education, every school in the Metroplex would have televised it. No one even bothers trying to pretend otherwise.

This is an ugly time to live in America. There are good people in our communities, but they're not speaking up, defending our better principles or challenging the sad elements that perpetrate outrages. Writer Albert Camus once said that evil in the world almost always stems from ignorance, and that good intentions may do as much harm as malevolence if they lack understanding.

The decision to prohibit the broadcast of President Obama's education speech in local schools was malevolent and the rationale behind it was clearly rooted in a lack of understanding. The vilification and dehumanization of our president is ignorant and dangerous. The racist indoctrination of our children is evil and loathsome.

Why is it being tolerated?

Why are we condoning Jim Crow tactics by our school officials and the rhetoric of lynching by media pundits and politicians?

The current hostilities go beyond sour grapes and unpopular

policy proposals. When malcontents attend political forums with guns, it's not just a Second Amendment stunt; it's a KKK tactic. When my son's classmates believe our president is an agent of Armageddon, Aledo becomes Salem, Massachusetts, in 1692. And when rabid tea-baggers hang politicians in effigy, it's no longer the twenty-first century. It's November in Dallas, circa 1963.

Tolerance, Dude

Fort Worth Weekly • *July 1, 2009*

The day after abortion doctor George Tiller was gunned down by a religious zealot, I was sitting on my couch watching one of my favorite high school movies, 80s classic *Fast Times at Ridgemont High*. A major character in *Fast Times* gets an abortion, but that's not what jumped out at me. It was actually the crude wisdom of Sean Penn's pothead icon "Jeff Spicoli" that grabbed my attention, because it highlighted the ignorance of religious activists all over this country.

The scene I refer to occurs late in the movie, when Spicoli is cornered at home by his history teacher, "Mr. Hand." Hand has decided that Spicoli owes him some of his free time because Spicoli wasted so much class time at school. They go over several lessons, the last of which addresses Thomas Jefferson's general intent in writing the *Declaration of Independence*. Spicoli concludes: "What Jefferson was saying was, Hey! You know, we left this England place 'cause it was bogus . . . so if we don't get some new rules ourselves, pronto, we'll just be bogus, too."

Amen, brother.

These days much is said about our nation having been founded upon religious principles. Legions of Christian leaders hold this perception up as justification for blurring the lines that separate church and state. And a large number of true believers feel the problem with America is that it has strayed too far from its religious roots. Both notions are based on bleary recollections of this nation's beginnings.

Religious conformity and standard observances of established church doctrine were never the chief impetus for our American genesis. In fact, quite the opposite was true. The folks that packed into the *Mayflower*, crossed the Atlantic and braved this new world, were religious rebels fleeing oppression and persecution. In Britain, they faced fines, imprisonment and execution for their religious views. The sanctimonious majority demanded that they adhere to the Church of England's prescribed values, morals and method of worship. Our early forebears refused and fled here so they could pursue their faith as they pleased. They came here to create communities based on religious freedom. The Founding Fathers shared these ideals and made sure the United States Constitution fostered a society based on religious freedom and tolerance.

Today, the thing that too many religious folks don't get is that when they attempt to legislate their morality and cram their belief systems down our throats, they don't champion the ideals and principles of the brave souls who started this nation; they embody the spiritual tyranny we came here to escape.

If you don't think evolution should be taught in our schools, fine. Home-school your anthropoid offspring or send them to a religious academy—but don't deny the rest of our children a solid foundation in science.

If you think a woman's place is in the home, that she should be the humble, unquestioning servant of her husband, so be it. But don't ask the rest of us to set our watch back two millennia.

If you don't think abortion is a choice a woman should have a right to make, okay. Write your local congressman. You're entitled to your opinion; just don't express it with guns or explosives.

If you think homosexuality is a choice, a sin or, as the Good Book puts it, an abomination, fine. Stop watching *Ellen*, never visit the Sistine Chapel, be wary of the FBI (a raging queer made it what it is today) and avoid eating shrimp, crawfish and lobster. Like homosexuality, the Bible condemns the consumption of crustaceans as an abomination in the eyes of the Lord (Leviticus 11;10-12).

In this country—whether we like it or not—being backwards, uninformed and intentionally or unintentionally ignorant is every man and woman's God-given right. The rest of us may think it's bogus, but we must respect their freedom to believe and measure righteousness as they see fit.

It's simply unfortunate that a chronic stoner has a better grasp of American history than so many of the faithful.

Reaping "Something Good"
from the Act of Rape?

Dissident Voice • *October 25, 2012*

These days, it's true. There's no telling what might come out a Republican's mouth.

Indiana Republican Senate candidate Richard Mourdock's recent suggestion that pregnancies resulting from rape should not be terminated because they comprise "something good that God intended to happen" says something really scary about a lot of Republicans and church folk.

First, it's blatantly insensitive. I wonder if Mourdock has daughters and how he would feel if his daughter was raped. I strain my brain to imagine reasonable words to console the poor girl and convince her to bring her assailant's offspring to term. I can come up with none. Perhaps they offer a class for it at Mourdock's church.

Second, it reveals a man devoid of empathy. If Mourdock were a woman or, more specifically, a raped, suddenly pregnant woman, would he still defend this stance? If he were a raped high school girl, would he quit school or put it on the backburner to care for his rapist's baby? If he were a raped college girl, would he drop some classes or take a few semesters off to care for his assailant's child? If he were a woman who already had children and a husband, would he have the child and realistically be able to love it as much as the fruits of legitimate wedlock? And what kind of situation would it create for the estranged husband?

And third, if God intended for Mourdock's daughter or his granddaughter or his wife or his mother or his niece to be raped and have her attacker's baby, how could this preordained act be considered a crime? God is, I'm told, incapable of evil. And if He intended for a woman to be raped, the rape must have been permitted or perpetuated with a greater good in mind. Would the rape be considered a benevolent assault?

Family values folks stress two-parent households; perhaps a rapist should only be punished if the female aborts the fruit of the defilement. Would pro-life folks advocate freeing the rapist if a woman impregnated via rape carries the "good" resulting from the assault to term? So he could get a job to support it and teach it to play catch?

Heck, regardless of whether the rapist is charged, convicted, acquitted or patted on the back for his role in this "intended" and therefore blessed pregnancy; the rapist would clearly be awarded standard parental and visitation rights–right?

And if the government took up and legislated Mourdock's morality in terms of rape, would then the government not be responsible for helping support the rapist's offspring if he was convicted and sent to prison?

I suppose there is a precedent for Mourdock's stance in Christianity. The Virgin Mary probably set the proper example. Technically speaking, she wasn't assaulted, but she was impregnated without consent. And she bore her impregnator's Son without question or complaint. Should contemporary victims of rape look to the Virgin Mary's example?

I know God works in mysterious ways, but is the patriarchal, nonsensical gibberish the Republicans keep peddling really an example of God's work or just the latest in their recent history of sexism and reproductive oppression?

And speaking of 'isms, does anyone really think the lily white mouthpieces for anti-abortion doctrines would really pitch such a fuss if most of the women having abortions were poor Hispanic or African-American females instead of white females? Women's access to birth control and the resultant economic mobility have clearly curbed Caucasian propagation trends in this country. Is white population resurgence the dirty secret behind limiting reproductive freedoms?

We all know the catchphrases.

Trans-vaginal ultra-sounds.

Just put an aspirin between your knees.

No exceptions for the mother.

No exceptions for rape.

The female body is naturally capable of terminating unwanted pregnancies.

The stuff coming out of many faithful Republican's mouths these days is downright disturbing.

Do they know what century it is? Are there any limits to their unabashed creepiness?

What will they say next?

Today the Pond, Tomorrow the World

The Paper of South Texas • March 4, 2007

One of the first movies I ever saw at a Texas drive-in theatre was a horror flick called *Frogs*. It was a wacked-out, B-movie gem released in 1972. The one-sheet featured a toad with a dead human hand in its mouth. The tag line read: *TODAY the pond! TOMORROW the World!*

The protagonists, literally led by frogs, were a band of indignant amphibians, reptiles, birds and insects who were fed up with human pollution and bent on taking matters into their own hands (or, in this case, claws, paws, etc.). The antagonists were—you guessed it—humans, led by a Dick Cheney-esque millionaire who was poisoning the surrounding ecosystem and trying to exterminate the strains of the local wildlife that he found annoying. A young Sam Elliott played a landscape photographer who warns the millionaire (and others) of their eco-folly and eventually leads the survivors of the zoological onslaught to safety. The best line of the movie is Elliott's deadpan interrogative as the strange deaths of his human cohorts mount: "What if nature were trying to get back at us?"

The movie wasn't Oscar material, but the *Twilight Zone* implications of the plot are worth considering.

What if Mother Nature did finally decide she'd had enough?

Would we be afforded any mercy?

Do we deserve mercy?

Deep down, I think we all know the answer. If biological or, for that matter, planetary justice was meted out tomorrow, the genocide of humanity would not be uncalled for. We are consuming ourselves toward oblivion and extirpating everything in our path.

We are destroying our habitat and ecosystem, and the rest of the members of the animal kingdom are just innocent bystanders.

Our progress has led to their marginality. Our extravagances are leading to their extinction.

Clearly, we must be stopped.

But do we have the necessary wisdom and willpower to stop ourselves? Do we have the discipline to limit our indulgences, stymie our greed and share the planet with the rest of the creatures that are trying to survive our existential intemperance? Do we have the fortitude to covet less and share more?

More often than not, the answers are *no, no* and *no*.

We want that Hummer, that Escalade. We have to have that four-wheeler, that jet-ski, that fifth TV. We need air conditioning, clothes dryers, dishwashers, power windows and garage door openers.

The most pressing challenge left to us as a species—for my generation, your generation and future generations—is (and will be) whether we can learn to control ourselves. Can we really learn to conserve? Can we live in harmony with the planet and our co-inhabitants? Can we achieve a balance?

If we can't or simply won't, Mother Nature should drop the hammer. Killer bees, fowl-borne viruses, swarms, stampedes, rodent-introduced plagues, parasitic bacteria, super-fungi, giant ants, piranha, Godzilla—whatever it takes.

It'll be the insects' turn. Or another primate's. It's difficult to say if they'll fare better than us, but they'd be hard-pressed to do any worse.

You probably aren't taking me seriously, but you should. A day of reckoning approaches.

And yesterday I saw a horny toad with a red beret barking orders into a cell phone.

Open Letter to
Rabbi Adam Jacobs and the Christian, Jewish, and Muslim Communities

Dissident Voice • February 21, 2011

In Rabbi Adam Jacobs' "Open Letter to the Atheist Community" a few years back, he suggested that there were no "true atheists" because the "totality of the universe" is unknowable, therefore it would be impossible to definitively prove that God doesn't exist. Jacobs also posited that Atheism was more a statement of principle than a cogent belief system; I say it's neither. I say it's a process. I say it's a mission.

The adjective "atypical" means "not typical." A condition, event or stance of "atypicality" does not mean "typicality" (or a "type") does not exist or that the state of being "typical" is impossible. It simply means a condition, an event or a stance is characterized by "atypicality." The same could be said of the adjectival term "apolitical."

The adjective "atheist," therefore, means "not theist." And an "Atheist" is simply not a Theist.

Atheism, then, is simply an existence not characterized by—or, in most of our cases, susceptible to—Theism. The onus to prove whether or not God, Allah, Jehovah, Yahweh, Elohim, etc. exists is completely irrelevant. If God, Allah, Jehovah or Yahweh do exist, We're not fans.

BELIEVERS: I am not insulting your god or assailing your fealty. I'm simply not on board.

To demonstrate my point, let me give you an example involving God in the Christian sense from the Book of Genesis.

I will readily admit that I'm not the smartest person around, but I know this: if I put cookies in several different cookie jars and tell my kids that the cookies in one jar contain the knowledge of good and evil and that they can partake of the cookies in any jar in the pantry except the ones from the cookie jar of good and evil, then—even if I put that jar on the highest shelf—my children are eventually (if not immediately) going to reach for the cookies in the forbidden cookie jar.

Any good parent probably understands this.

What kind of parent would scold a child after purposefully setting a trap and then watching the child fall into it? What kind of parent would exile his children from his grace because they fell into the trap he or she set for them?

I may not be the smartest person in the world or the best parent but, in this particular respect, I'm arguably smarter than God. And I wouldn't have done what He supposedly did to His children even if the staging and subsequent results achieved the desired effect.

The therapeutic entity (or pseudo-entity) that Christians refer to as the Divine Author is clearly something of a mixed bag. He reportedly made the sun, the moon and the stars, but had no grasp of human nature even though we were supposedly made in His image. It doesn't make sense. An omnipotent being would, well, be omnipotent.

If God was or is truly omnipotent, shame on Him. Omnipotence implies infallibility. Infallibility precludes causal error. That means God knew He was setting up Adam and Eve and manipulated them to fail and then punished them for failing.

The lesson to be taken from the exercise is that God expects blind, abject obedience. No more, no less. And if this was God's plan for us all along, He shouldn't have bothered with humanity at all.

Perhaps my thought processes border on incivility, but I believe that (1) no reasonable creator would require abject obedience of any organism, (2) no responsible creator would grant any single species ipso facto dominion over all others (any more than He would favor one people, place or faith over another) and (3) no relevant, competent creator would value rote reverence and voluntary meekness over thoughtful query and existential initiative.

In my admittedly fallible mind, this leaves us with two possibilities: (A) The entire concept of God is a giant fraud and may comprise the greatest lie ever told or (B) God is imperfect and possibly incompetent.

I would certainly never presume to speak for all Atheists, but I have to say this: if God exists, I'm not impressed and I don't want Him on my side. His taste in "chosen" peoples and cultures is lacking and His intentions are suspect.

My mission, then, as an Atheist, is not to prove or disprove His existence to His followers. It's simply to discourage and dissuade them from trying to define, limit or marginalize my existence any more than they already have.

This applies to Muslims and Jews as well.

It's typical to believe that life on this planet began with a desert god; and it's typical to think the world will end according to a desert religion. But the intellectual landscape for some of us is not so barren.

True Wealth

Fort Worth Weekly • *March 10, 2010*

The other day my son tried a new tack to get out of going to school. He said he didn't like his school because it was too hard. He said "normal" schools were easier, and he wanted to go to a normal school.

I told him I had gone to the same school when I was his age and that I didn't recall its being that difficult, especially when I worked at it. He conceded that I had gone to the same "hard" school that he does and pointed out that I had also gone to college—*but look where I was working now.*

Ouch.

And this coming from a ten-year-old.

I knew he was just trying to be clever and get out of going to class that day, but it still stung. I graduated from college with honors, and I work in construction. But way leads on to way, and things are not always what they seem.

At age twenty-seven, I had a lucrative white-collar job with a percentage of the overall profits. I got paid a lot for doing a little and certainly nothing of any consequence. I despised the work and had no respect for the corporate entity that employed me. Whether virtue or defect, something in me insisted that there was more to life than corporate drudgery and that no matter how much they paid me, the job would still be pointless and existentially demeaning.

I took a leave of absence and backpacked through Europe. I returned a few months later with shoulder-length dreadlocks and a better outlook. I felt ten-years younger and resolved then not to reduce myself to any form of white-collar, corporate degradation ever again.

How could I explain that to my son? I had no regrets, but he was too young to understand.

When I was in college, I had as much fun as the next student, but I also got an education. I read the works of great thinkers, and I examined the paths and principles of some of humanity's most important heroes and visionaries. Most of what I learned indicated that we had gone astray.

I don't want to shock Middle America, but the best application of a college education is not to make piles of money. It's to be educated.

There are lots of folks going to college these days, but few are getting an education. In fact, if you duck off into curricula like those offered in business departments, you may not even be exposed to a real education, much less educated You can just learn how to shuffle and count money and lay people off.

A good education tells you that dollar signs are not the most important thing in the world. A good education tells you that the corporatization of America is making a mockery of our defining ideals. A good education tells you that no CEO, movie star, or professional athlete is important enough to be making a thousand times more than whoever's working the drive-through window at McDonald's—because no one is that special.

Now, at forty-three, I admit I didn't win all my battles, and every year I find less and less energy to resist what I know in every cell of my being is an undesirable existence. But I can say I tried.

The choices I made may not make sense to my son now, but maybe when he's twenty-seven (or forty-three) he'll understand. He'll make different choices, and that's fine. In the end, you can't tell anyone how to live, not even your own son. All you can do is make a statement with your existence. My life may not be impressive to him right now, but he doesn't want for much, and it's easier for me to look myself in the mirror than it would have been if I had remained a corporate cog.

When I was young, people used to say, "There's the way things are and there's the way things should be." Someday, like me, my son will have to decide whether it's better to spend his life struggling for the way things should be or settling for how they are.

Settling might net you lots of dollar signs. But struggling may lead to truer wealth.

Groovy National Product

Fort Worth Weekly • *January 17, 2007*

Oh beautiful for spacious skies, for emerald waves of . . . cannabis?

OK, I'm sorry. I couldn't help it. It's just the first thing that came to mind when I heard "pot" had finally hit the big time in this country.

According to public policy analyst Jon Gettman, marijuana is now America's largest cash crop. In a report released in December, Gettman concluded that the United States produces 10,000 metric tons of wacky-tobacky annually. That's an estimated $35 billion worth of "weed," "reefer," or "ganja."

And we thought the war in Iraq was going badly.

We've been losing the war there for only a year or so. We've been losing the War on Drugs for twenty years.

Legions of folks are going to fret and shake their heads in disbelief. But hey, it's no big deal. So what if we produce five times as much weed as the wheat we harvest, three times as much reefer as the hay we make, and one and a half times as much ganja as the corn we grow. We're capitalists, baby. And pot is the current heavyweight of our "fruited" plains. It's just the way of things. Our amber waves of grain simply got downsized.

I know what you're thinking.

This isn't acceptable. We've gotta put a stop to this.

I commend your resolve, but it may be misplaced.

I don't smoke pot. It was never my thing. But I've known a few folks that were partial to it, and they weren't bad people. They didn't hurt anybody or push anybody around. And they weren't belligerent or out of control or a danger to themselves.

I can't say that for many of the drinkers I know. If you overindulge in pot, you laugh too much and drive slow. If you overindulge in alcohol, you get loud and rambunctious and run people off the road.

Ever hear of someone choking to death on their own vomit because of pot poisoning? Alcohol is a hundred times more dangerous than pot. And the nicotine in a cigarette is much more addictive. So why agonize over homegrown bud?

It even has medicinal properties. Marijuana alleviates the nausea caused by chemotherapy and helps reduce weight loss caused by AIDS. It eases the chronic pain that's associated with multiple sclerosis and cancer. It reduces the debilitating effects of glaucoma. Researchers are finding productive uses for marijuana all the time.

Of course it's also been proven to impair memory, diminish attention span, and retard cognitive processes, but that doesn't make it any more hazardous than television.

According to recent Census Bureau data, the average American spends four hours in front of a TV per day. If you plop yourself down in front of the tube for four hours every day, you're at least as unproductive as a pothead. And you probably get the munchies. And you probably have no particular urge to accomplish anything of consequence. So what's the difference between a television addict and a pot smoker?

At least potheads are paranoid. Television addicts nod along with everything they see on the tube. I'd rather hang out with a burned-out dope-smoker than a feeble-minded tube rube any day.

Truth be told, every dime bag could have a silver lining. Fewer and fewer folks want American beef. And no one seems interested in buying our cars. If pot was legalized, regulated, and taxed, it could turn into a real cash cow. It could turn out to be something that people around the world are more interested in buying than our guns. And if fewer folks had our guns, we'd have less dictators to depose.

In fact, if pot replaced weaponry as our most profitable export, the wars would probably be over. The world would be safer, and our economy could be based on something besides blood or oil.

Dude. How excellent would that be?

Condoms Optional: Getting Fracked by the Oil and Gas Industry in North Texas

Dissident Voice • *October 20, 2010*

I chuckled out loud the other day when I heard that a "No-hooker" zone in Arlington was rejected by the city council and Mayor Robert Cluck. I know Arlington Police Chief Theron Bowan's request for this exclusionary section was an earnest attempt to address the prostitution problem that has sprung up around Rangers Ballpark and Cowboy Stadium, but the whole measure was pricelessly ironic.

If you look up the meaning of the verb form of "prostitute" in the dictionary, you'll find two definitions: 1) to sell the services of oneself (or another) for purposes of sexual intercourse; 2) to sell oneself, one's artistic or moral integrity, etc., for low or unworthy purposes.

We like to forget that second denotation in Capitalist society. It hits too close to home. Who are we to question the system? Who are we to question how other folks' livings are made?

The problem with not asking these questions in our community is that we also like to believe that criminality is punished and justice is at least a desired goal.

Prostitution is illegal and I have no problem with Chief Bowman or the City of Arlington accosting, arresting and prosecuting hookers in what's come to be known as "prostitution central" in the city's entertainment district; but it's like chasing a pimply-faced, emo drop-out with a half-ounce of pot down a dark alley instead of seizing a drug cartel kingpin in broad daylight.

The biggest whore in Arlington is not an abused, down-on-her-luck prostitute, trying to make some extra cash or fund her coke habit. It's Republican Congressman Joe Barton. Since early 2009, he's been the U.S. House of Representatives' biggest recipient of contributions from the oil and gas industry, approaching $2,000,000 in "love" money. And he's loved them long time.

Barton has been in on or lead every attack on repeated federal and local attempts to regulate the pollutants that the oil and gas folks are pumping into our atmosphere and our water supply and, at the height of the BP Spill hearings, he even apologized to former BP president Tony Hayward for having to endure the criticism and grievances aired by fellow congressmen who don't put price tags on their virtue or conscience. And now, if the Republicans retake the majority in the House, that beady-eyed little strumpet will be trying to sell his "wares" as Chairman of the House Energy and Commerce Committee.

But the Arlington cat house offices of Congressman Joe Barton are not Tarrant County's only den of obscene wantonness. Of the approximately 43,000 zip codes that make up these United States, the 76102 zip code of downtown Fort Worth leads the nation in political contributions from the same high class clients that associate with Barton: the oil and gas industry.

Regular 76102 "Johns" include XTO Energy, Chesapeake Energy, Range Resources, Titan Operating and Quicksilver Resources and over $250,000 in "love" money has made it into federal coffers from this area in this election cycle, $225,000 of which was given to the oil and gas industry's favorite "escort," the Republican Party.

I don't know about you, but where I come from a quarter of a million dollars pays for a whole lotta' "fracking." And that's what the lechers downtown are paying for. They want to drill the Barnett Shale cheaply and discreetly, and they don't want the going rates for the "tricks" they enjoy raised or the mess they make fussed about. They like a "Wham-Bam-Thank-You-Ma'am!" arrangement that allows them to get in and out without attracting too much attention.

So I don't want to hear about Arlington police officers rousting small-time hookers around Cowboy Stadium unless some version of a federal vice squad is going to shake down Barton or give the "johns" of 76102 the Hugh Grant treatment. They operate the biggest rings of prostitution in our community and comprise the most illicit presence in our daily lives.

Atlas Slacked (and So Should We)

Dissident Voice • *February 16, 2011*

I have no money, no resources, no hopes. I am the happiest man alive.

Thus spake Henry Miller on the first page of his first book, *Tropic of Cancer*, in 1934—no doubt one of the reasons it was banned from publication in the United States until 1961. Miller was a square wheel and not the kind of influence a country trying to get things rolling after a Great Depression wanted folks exposed to. The book was deemed pornographic as well, but the social criticism was more risqué than the gratuitous sex.

Today, as we continue to work our way out of the Great Recession, many of Miller's *Cancer* sentiments still ring true as we mark the fiftieth-anniversary of its appearance on our shores. Materialism is unwise. Over-consumption is destructive. And the most recent incarnation of American Capitalism is simply a diagonally slit wrist that we're watching bleed out.

Deep down, we all know this, but we can't seem to muster the craw or the courage to square our wheels. It makes me think back to a time and place in my life when people tried.

It was Austin, Texas, in the early 1990s. I lived on my friend Jerry's couch in a duplex in Hyde Park for nine months. I kept odd jobs and odder hours, usually scheduled around manic chess marathons and bleary-eyed, late-night philosophical volleys. The debates always started with a lob, but three hours later we were both trying to maintain serve with obscure, paraphrased excerpts from Nietzsche or clever parries from Kierkegaard, Camus or Sartre.

Jerry had an uncanny knowledge of local happy hours at restaurants that offered free finger foods for the thirsty souls that frequented their establishments to imbibe alcohol. So we would show up, buy one beer each and then just eat; it was a nice dinner one to three days a week.

When the hinges of our toilet seat broke off, we simply hung the lid on the bathroom door. Using our water closet involved placing the lid on the toilet bowl and balancing yourself.

I barely had a broken pot to piss in and it was one of the happiest times in my life. I didn't have a mortgage or car payments or credit cards. I wasn't prostituting myself in some pathetic, cubicled slog and I wasn't a stock-optioned salary-slave with no place to go but up the arse of a corporate colossus slinking after ill-gotten profit margins.

I was free. I could loaf. And I could sit still and think.

Richard Linklater's *Slacker* touched on the phenomena, but conveyed the weirder aspects of the process more than the wisdom. In fact, the movie reinforced the stereotype that a "slacker" was a young adult whose existence was characterized by apathy, lack of ambition and general aimlessness. The derogatory connotations masked the profounder aspects of what was really happening. We weren't apathetic or lazy or aimless; we just had serious reservations about the catalogue of ways people are forced to demean themselves for money.

Austin in the early 1990s was a place where "Atlases" came to shrug. Moms and dads across the state were sending their kids off to UT or Southwest Texas State University for vocational training, but some of the stuff in some of the books was leaving an impression. And a significant number of students theretofore scheduled to become normal, traditionally successful yuppies were garnering (1) levels of awareness that were counterproductive, (2) penchants for self-examination that were downright dangerous and (3) a contrarian vein that approached anarchy.

Resignation, obsequiousness and utter convention were out. Herman Hesse's *Steppenwolf* had observed that to think was to undermine and, with our educations in hand, that's exactly what we did. We didn't have much practice and our non-conformist leanings were almost unanimously discouraged by real "grown-ups," but once we thought for ourselves for a summery instant we realized the entire phony system wasn't worth engaging in, struggling for or reducing ourselves to. So we stayed in Austin and held out as long as we could (but not nearly long enough).

I bring this up because my happy "shrug" in Austin comes to mind a lot lately, especially when I see Tea Partiers hold up signs that say "Who is John Galt?" For the record, I like Ayn Rand, but she made a mistake in *Atlas Shrugged* when she assumed that talented folks and great innovators would automatically be capitalists. Rand had too much reverence for the "system" and naively suggested that Capitalist Atlases might shrug, but that's never been the case-because they always benefited too much from the "system." Rand might as well have titled the book "Robber-Barron Shrugged" or "Industrialist Shrugged" or "When Corporations Shrug."

History clearly suggests that the "shruggers" were never members of the upper Capitalist caste. They were hardscrabble types, common people, beset-upon folks that refused to surrender to the robber-barons, industrialists and corporatists who solemnly and repeatedly endeavored to relegate them to Capitalism's dirty, secret byproduct: a powerless heap of the collaterally damaged and chronically disenfranchised (also known as the middle and lower classes).

So take notes, Ayn.

A union work stoppage is John Galt.

A strain of talented college graduates refusing to become cogs in a soul-crushing, environment-ravaging corporate machine is John Galt.

And a collection of Egyptian protestors speaking truth to power in Tahir Square is also John Galt.

Our country is in trouble because we don't believe in America anymore. And we shouldn't. But not because our president is black or because our government is too big or we pay too many taxes. It's because we no longer operate under the precept of collective self-interest. We have self-interest down to a science and regard self-indulgence as the fulfillment of the American Dream. But "collective" no longer has a place in the equation because it's an unpleasantness that the have-mores and the have-mosts pay legions of lawmakers and lobbyists to help them avoid. Then they enthusiastically hail unrestrained, unregulated free markets as the amazing cure-all for our times and utilize their government-sanctioned privileges to remove the third, fourth, fifth, sixth and seventh rung on every ten-foot stretch of the socioeconomic ladder so that we are systemically and perpetually beholden to them if we are inclined to climb.

The ladder is still navigable if you're connected, related, incredibly lucky or prepared to jump real high when they tell you to—but if you question their authority or resent their entitlement you're an extremist, a radical or an insurrectionist who must be quashed.

As I think Henry Miller would have more colorfully noted, unrestrained capitalism, corporatism, materialism and our destructive way of life in general are not too big to fail and we're not so small that we won't survive when they do.

The have-mores and the have-mosts who control everything in this country are a conglomerate version of Hosni Mubarak. Different crime scene, different M.O., but same criminality. And obligatorily shouldering their burden simply makes us enablers.

So become a square wheel. Slack a little. Take some time and think.

The mortgage, the car and the flat-screen can wait.

There's always surrender. But it should be a last resort. Not our chief priority.

Johnny Got His Pills

Fort Worth Weekly • *October 27, 2010*

After U.S. Army Sgt. Douglas Hale, Jr. finished fifteen months in Iraq for his second combat tour, it was obvious that things in his life had gone awry. In 2007, he was diagnosed with severe depression and post-traumatic stress disorder. He began drinking heavily and his marriage fell apart. In early 2009, Hale abandoned his post at Fort Hood. This past May, he was arrested for being absent without leave and returned to Fort Hood. Before the month was out, he tried to kill himself.

The Army sent Hale for treatment at a psychiatric hospital in Denton, and it seemed to help. He spent the 4th of July weekend with his mother and she drove him back to Fort Hood on July 5th. On July 6th, his mother received a text message from him that said "I love you mom im so sorry I hope u and family and god can forgive me." She immediately contacted Army officials at Fort Hood and started driving back. But Hale had already shot himself in the head.

Our Army brass is looking for answers regarding the suicides of soldiers like Hale, but not right under their noses. War is insane. It isn't hell; it's a planned, coordinated communal psychosis. If you take a normal, all-American boy or girl and plop them down in a psychotic situation for months and years at a time, tour after tour, psychosis or extreme disturbance are predictable responses. And they can lead to suicide. Especially when the nation who sent these men and women into harm's way still hasn't clearly justified why this madness was necessary. It's hard enough to maintain your sanity in a war zone when you're fighting the good fight. But when you're risking your life or limbs or sanity simply to fulfill the "wartime president" fantasy of an imbecilic, oil fund aristocrat or to enable a rich, pasty-faced assembly of stuffed shirts to appear "tough" on terrorism, your outlook on things isn't going to be positive. Or healthy.

I read an AP piece in the newspaper the other day that suggested that one of Big Pharma's wonder drugs was killing American GIs. It said that many of the soldiers serving in and returning home from the wars in Afghanistan and Iraq were taking a drug called Seroquel to help them deal with chronic restlessness, severe insomnia and constant nightmares. If I was a soldier this might have made me laugh.

Seroquel is a "potent anti-psychotic." Instead of reducing combat tours to reasonable time frames, limiting the number of tours a soldier should have to endure or simply removing unstable soldiers from the psychotic environment of these ill-conceived wars indefinitely, the U.S. Military is apparently using our men and women in uniform as guinea pigs for a soldier's-little-helper pill that will supposedly desensitize them to the insanity.

It doesn't cure the psychosis. It simple allows unstable soldiers to function within the insanity without being terribly bothered by it. And when you combine Seroquel with antidepressants and anti-anxiety drugs—something military officials suggest is an acceptable "standard of care" for soldiers or veterans suffering from post-traumatic stress disorder—any semblance of normal sentience is truncated to the point where they walk around in a cognitive fog or detached stupor.

In this regard, isn't the U.S. Military's pharmaceutical attempt to abridge the humanity of our soldiers its own form of insanity? If you have to give someone a "potent anti-psychotic" to help them deal with what they're doing or what they've done for you or God or country—then there's obviously something wrong with what you're asking them to do. It reminds me of perhaps the grimmest excerpt from Erich Maria Remarque's *All Quiet on the Western Front*: "We were eighteen and had begun to love life and the world; and we had to shoot it to pieces. The first bomb, the first explosion, burst in our hearts."

Conveniently, Seroquel is more than just one of the military's most frequently prescribed drugs. It's also the fifth best-selling drug in the nation. So if our psychotic naivete and ignorance ever start to really get to us, we can always knock them back with a brain-fuddling stupefacient. In fact, we've already been at it.

In 2008, American emergency rooms treated a million people for abusing prescription drugs and over-the-counter medicines, roughly the same number of folks our ERs treated for heroin and cocaine overdoses or abuses of other illegal drugs—and this number doesn't even factor in alcohol. We're taking the edge off our insanity any way we can. The only war more stupid and psychotic than the one in Iraq was the one on drugs. But it's been going on so long its mention no longer even penetrates our daze.

The military-pharmaceutical complex is making a killing or, more specifically, making a fortune off the folks we've asked to do the killing—and the rest of us. They dope our unruly kids, they dope the young men and women fighting in and returning home from the war. They dope the rest of us right here at home for being sick of wars overseas and fearful of war on the Middle and Lower Classes. And the dope those disgusted by Capitalist expediency and dreading the reckonings to come and who are ashamed of our own sad, national shadow.

A Drive-By

Dissident Voice • *August 7, 2010*

So last week I'm sitting at the Lowdon Track and Field Complex at Texas Christian University watching my daughter and her teammates prepare for the upcoming Texas Amateur Athletic Federation's State Track and Field Championships. Her coach is working them hard, even in the summer heat. They're running curves and practicing hand-offs. Another track club is there as well, and some TCU sprinters. The athletes are starting to get into a groove and coaches and parents alike are admiring the vibe and quietly jazzed by the speed and effort of the kids, whether they're elementary, junior high, high school or college students.

Then a white, compact sedan drives by, heading north on Berry Street (where it runs parallel to the first straightaway of the track) and a young white male hangs out the passenger-door window and yells "Nigggggers!" at the top of his lungs.

At first, I'm not sure what I heard. This is, after all, the twenty-first century.

But I heard right. The plural version of the N-word, loud and proud. And I see in some of the other parents' faces that they heard it too. It makes me angry. And then I'm just embarrassed.

You see, most of the other parents were black. I'm white. The bumpkins behind the drive-by were one of me.

In the world of serious track, white folks are the minority and we're hard not to notice. We try to fit in, but sometimes it's difficult—especially when Caucasoid clowns are howling racial slurs.

There was nothing to be done about it. We shook our heads and turned back to our children. The incident wasn't anything the black parents and black kids hadn't experienced before, so they took it in stride. But it stuck in my mind.

When those racist goons got to where they were going, did they yuk it up, proud of themselves, high-fives all around? Did they salute a Confederate flag back at their frat house or a Nazi swastika in their flat? Did they revel in "white" pride?

In the bigger picture, our new mixed president seems to have reminded a lot of white folks of their white pride. Ignorant, closet racists who might otherwise have never been heard from or ever openly emitted a racist chirp have come out of the woodwork because their bigotry is now legitimate. The Republican tea partyers sanction it under the guise of "taking their country back." Rush Limbaugh legitimizes it practically every time he opens his mouth. And it's no accident that right-wing operatives like Andrew Breitbart are stoking the inanity behind racial prejudice and racial paranoia when they trumpet distortions of the New Black Panther "polling place" incident and outright lies about upstanding black Americans like Shirley Sherrod.

At this historical moment, the stars are curiously aligned for racists in the same way they aligned for Joe McCarthy (a precursor to contemporary Neocons) during the Red Scare. Riding a wave of gullibility, ignorance and xenophobia, McCarthy created, fueled and legitimized a communal neurosis that passed through the American ranks of the un- and ill-informed like it was being spread by Paul Revere. But, thankfully—*Fox News* notwithstanding—racial paranoia will end the same way Communist paranoia did: with the folks behind it having to abandon their abuses of others, reduced simply to abusing themselves until obscurity overtakes them or small religious colleges offer them board seats or professorships.

Racists are not going to like hearing this, but their frenzy of idiocy is as understandable as it is ludicrous. The sad truth is it's the only weapon they have against irrelevance.

Ultimately, that's what Andrew Breitbart, Rush Limbaugh and the bumpkins who yelled a racial epithet at our track practice are. Irrelevant. The country is moving on. The ulterior motives behind their campaigns against President Obama are obvious. And the racist jabs and jibes will simply comprise a long and stubborn death rattle. Their impunity is finished. Their imbecility is drawing to an end. The country isn't going to stay white anymore than it was going to stay slaveholding, McCartheistic or homophobic.

The bozos behind the drive-by are ugly relics, living breathing reminders of a more obtuse, unjust time that too many white folks in this country still hold dear. A time when pasty-complexioned, grey-haired conservative presidents told them they were better than everyone else and their paleness would prevail.

The world is changing and white folks' daydream of supremacy is evaporating as fast as the fresh water supply. The myths that suggest one skin color, one people or one religion is better than the rest have been proven to be as illogical and unhealthy as fossil-fuel dependence. And, truth be told, the reign of the white guy has been about as good for the planet as Capitalism.

Someday this will dawn on us.

But in the meanwhile, saner folks will probably have to endure a billion more slurs, a dozen more political shootings, a few more lily-white Janet Brewers or Rush Limbaughs and perhaps another George Armstrong Custer.

Too many of us are still a little slow.

Oil to Dry Our Tears?

Fort Worth Weekly • *September 23, 2009*

I have never seen the Sahara Desert, but someday I'd like to. My Uncle Jimmy made an unscheduled stop there twenty years ago, and it turned out to be his last.

On September 19, 1989, Uncle Jimmy hopped a plane to Paris in N'Djamena, Chad. He'd been working there for Exxon. The job was great until he was kidnapped and held hostage. Upon his release, he decided it was time to come home.

His flight, UTA 772, on a McDonnell Douglas DC-10 operating for French airline Union des Transports Aeriens, was only in the air for forty-six minutes. At a cruising altitude of 35,000 feet, a suitcase exploded and the plane broke up over the Tenere region of Niger.

The sudden break-up made the cabin temperature drop 129 degrees and the thin air caused Uncle Jimmy to experience hypoxia, perhaps even resulting in a black-out. But as the jet plummeted, the oxygen content grew and he was probably able to take one or two breaths before the fire caused by the explosion engulfed the wreckage and scorched his lungs. Then he asphyxiated until dead and the flames cooked him to a crisp.

When search crews found the crash a few hours later, Uncle Jimmy and his fellow travelers, including U.S. Ambassador to Chad Robert Pugh's wife, Bonnie, were still strapped into their seats and burnt black as coal. As the desert sands whispered around the debris, extremists groups began claiming responsibility for the act and the frantic relatives of the 170 victims aboard UTA 772 commenced a shedding of tears that probably matched the rainfall that had fallen in that part of the Sahara that year.

In the early 1980s, the United States and Libya wrangled several times in the Gulf of Sidra, culminating in the destruction of two Libyan SU-22 fighters by U.S. Navy jets on August 19, 1981. Libyan leader Muammar al-Gaddafi stewed for a while and then, on April 5, 1986, Libyan operatives bombed a West German discotheque, killing two U.S. servicemen and maiming sixty-three others. On April 16, 1986, President Reagan ordered retaliatory attacks against the Libyan capital of Tripoli and city of Benghazi, killing fifteen Libyans (including Gaddafi's fifteen-month-old adopted daughter) and wounding 100 others. On December 21, 1988, Libyan operatives blew up Pan Am 103 over Lockerbie, Scotland. And ten months later, they sabotaged UTA 772.

In 1999, six Libyans were tried and convicted in absentia at the Paris Assize Court for the bombing of UTA 772, but Libya denied any involvement. Later, Libya admitted culpability for the UTA 772 and Pan Am 103 bombings, but would not accept responsibility. Then, Gaddafi had a change of heart. The Libyan economy was sputtering and he realized Libya could profit by cozying up with the West.

After the overthrow of Saddam Hussein by U.S. forces, Gaddafi announced he had WMDS and allowed international inspectors into Libya. They found rudimentary weapons and destroyed them accordingly.

In 2003, Libya accepted responsibility for the Lockerbie Bombing and became the first state sponsor of terrorism to begin compensating the families of its victims. In 2004, U.S.-Libya relations were formally normalized. By March 2006, Gaddafi had a new lease on Western credibility and France was helping Libya develop a nuclear power program. In August 2007, D.C. District Judge Henry Kennedy found Libya directly responsible for the UTA 772 bombing and later, in January 2008, awarded $6 billion in damages to the families of the victims and owners of the airliner. Libya appealed this decision but, in late October 2008, agreed to pay $1.5 billion into a fund that would compensate U.S. victims of Pan Am 103 (the remaining 20% still owed on original compensation agreement), UTA 722, and the Berlin discotheque bombing. President George W. Bush then signed an executive order granting Libya immunity from further terrorism-related lawsuits.

Last month, August 17-18, U.S. Senators John McCain, Joseph Lieberman, Lindsey Graham and Susan Collins paid Libya a trade visit. Two days later, on August 20, Abdel Basset Ali al-Megrahi—the only Libyan ever imprisoned for the sabotage of Pan Am 103 or UTA 722—was released from Scottish custody due to terminal illness. Scottish compassion not-so-coincidentally also sweetened British (i.e., American) campaigns for billions in Libyan energy and defense contracts.

I know Libya's oil reserves number upwards of 40 billion barrels and the release of one dying terrorist is a small price to pay for increased fossil fuel access—but our acquiescence still sets a disturbing precedent. Twenty years from now if Osama Bin Laden presides over an oil-rich nation will we find it in our hearts to accept financial compensation for 9/11 and let bygones be bygones as we have in Gaddafi's case?

I think we all know the answer.

We're still oil and gas addicts and any addiction counselor will tell you that junkies like us would sell their grandmothers for a fix. In this case grandma was spared. We just betrayed the memories of folks like Uncle Jimmy and Bonnie Pugh and swallowed the indignation we harbored towards their murderers. But the more you do it, the less it hurts. After taking money for the first three hundred 9/11 victims, it would surely get easier. And by the time we received compensatory funds for the 2000th victim, Bin Laden would seem like an old fraternity buddy.

Much of the UTA 772 wreckage still sits where it landed, the major exception being the DC-10's right wing. In 2007, French relatives of the victims stood it up, encased the base in concrete and mounted a placard memorializing the victims. I'd like to see this monument someday, but when we acknowledged Libya as a friend and then obsequiously released al-Megrahi, that upright DC-10 wing in the desert became something less than a memorial.

If I finally make it to the Tenere region of the Sahara it won't be to gaze upon this tribute. It will be to remove the memorial placard and send it Libya.

Gaddafi deserves a receipt.

45 Luft Balloons
Dissident Voice • *July 25, 2008*

When Larry Walters was a child, he dreamed of flying. Like so many of us, his childhood aspirations initially eluded him. He wanted to join the Air Force, but his vision wasn't good enough. He became a truck driver instead, and his early dreams of flight were deferred until he decided to improvise.

He and his girlfriend bought helium tanks and forty-five weather balloons. They attached the balloons to a patio chair and filled them with helium. He packed a CB radio, sandwiches, drinks, a camera, a parachute and a pellet gun (which he intended to use to lower himself by shooting the balloons one-by-one). He expected to ascend to 100 feet and enjoy a little piece of the sky before coming down.

When Walters launched his lawn chair on July 2, 1982, the makeshift craft wildly exceeded expectations. Within seconds he was a UFO hovering at height of 16,000 feet. From his home in San Pedro, California he drifted several miles into controlled airspace near Long Beach Airport. He used his CB to alert air traffic controllers.

After forty-five minutes aloft, Walters began shooting the balloons and descending slowly. Near the ground, his dangling balloon cables got caught in a power line and caused a twenty-minute blackout in the area. When he touched down, he was immediately arrested by Long Beach police officers. Then, a regional FAA Safety Inspector was reported to have said "We know he broke some part of the Federal Aviation Act, and as soon as we decide which part it is, some type of charge will be filed."

When a reporter asked Walters why he did it, he said "A man can't just sit around."

Whenever I feel aggrieved by "standard operating procedures" or the typical pencil-neck rigamarole, I fondly recall Walters' feat.

Was it prudent or practical? *Definitely not.*

Was it ill-advised? *Perhaps.*

But that's the genius of it.

I'm tired of being consistent and reliable. I'm sick of being steady, solid and stable—i.e., predictable, sedentary and dull. Half the time I don't recognize myself. I'm hardly sentient. I travel hither and thither vaguely aware and vaguely interested, like a doomed automaton. And I know it wasn't always so.

What kind of life is it that we've built for ourselves that metaphysical inaction maintains a prominent role in our daily go of it? Is a culture that virtually commands we surrender to conformity, conservatism and cowering worth preserving? *What happened to us?*

Our better-adjusted friends and relatives will dismissively say we just "grew" up. But is that what it's really all about?

Over the last couple of decades, one of my dad's friends has repeatedly imparted an adage regarding this issue. He says if you're not a liberal when you're young, you have no heart; but if you're not a conservative when you're old, you have no brains.

I resent it every time I hear it. He states it like an unapproachable truism. I think it's a ridiculous cop-out.

If I'm not officially old, I'm on the cusp of being old and it seems to me that middle age and Golden-Year conservatism is not the product of brain presence (or prowess). No offense, but I think it's the result of stagnation, habit-clinging and general disengagement (not to mention a touch of cowardice.

Obviously, most young people have more energy, resilience and gumption than we thirty- and forty-somethings. But that's no excuse. They're less informed and less experienced. We don't abandon progressive movements and liberal principles because conservative ideology makes more sense to us. Our better angels simply run out of steam.

We give up on youth and youthful visions because we become complacent and lazy. We're bought off through our own indulgences and brought down by our own resignation. Then, instead of being critical of ourselves, we become critics of who we were, attempting to rationalize and justify what we've become.

Larry Walters didn't give up so easy. Instead of sitting around and settling in for the long, cozy mediocrity that awaits most of us, he reached for something radical and way-out. This is what's missing from the American Dream today. Even if we secure the means or possess the wherewithal to do something special or heroic or inspiring, we almost invariably fritter it away on paths or projects of less resistance and more traditional scale.

Electing a black man to the highest political office in the galaxy is a fine start, but we all have a long way to go. And it doesn't take much to put us on the right track. It's simply a matter of building something or planting something or stepping forward or refusing to step back or speaking out or taking a chance.

Where we're at isn't all there is; it's just what we've brought ourselves to.

Things could change overnight if we improvised and stopped sitting around.

. . . One Heterosexual Nation, Under God, With Liberty and Justice for Straight People

OpEdNews • *November 24, 2008*

The other day I found myself at a Veteran's Day observance that included the *Pledge of Allegiance*. I stood up, put my hand over my heart and recited the oath.

I have to admit that it had been awhile. At first, I didn't think I would remember the all the words; but I made it through.

Unfortunately, while saying the pledge, I had a troubling revelation.

The pledge was an empty promise. It spoke of ideals and rights that America doesn't represent. It affirmed lofty notions and high principles that we don't even try to live up to.

The original *Pledge of Allegiance* was written in 1892 by Francis Bellamy. A Baptist minister and Christian Socialist, Bellamy had originally considered using the words "equality" and "fraternity" in the salute, but deemed them too controversial because so many factions in our "indivisible" nation opposed equal rights for women and African Americans. And, though Bellamy was a minister, the early versions of the pledge were secular and did not include the words "under God." The phrase mandating that we prostrate ourselves and our nation before a Judeo-Christian deity wasn't introduced until June 14, 1954.

In its current form, the *Pledge of Allegiance* has been amended four times. It was originally composed with prevailing winds in mind and similarly revised along the way. As I recited the pledge on Veteran's Day, it occurred to me that it's time for another revision.

For starters, we don't constitute one nation united under God any more than we comprise one nation united under a red, white and blue barber pole. Beyond that, the term "divisible" far more accurately describes us than its exalted counterpart "indivisible." And all the "liberty and justice for all" malarkey—we shouldn't even go there.

Saying the *Pledge of Allegiance* always sounds nice, but reality doesn't rest in a cadence. It exists in our efforts to fulfill the ideals that the pledge affirms. If we're not working towards the fruition of those noble goals, the pledge is meaningless. And if any of us are disqualified or denied his or her right to pursue those ideals, our meritorious oath is hollow.

Here in Texas, the ignoble 2005 "Marriage Amendment" to the state constitution, which forbade the recognition of same-sex couples and prohibited any branch of government from offering them relationship-based benefits, denied a viable, productive segment of our community the application to and enjoyment of some very basic tenets of "liberty" and "justice." And the recent repeal of Proposition 8 in California was another glaring travesty. To grant our friends and neighbors a right and then take it away via mob rule clearly evidences the fact that we are perpetually "divisible," especially in regards to sexual orientation.

Ultimately, our so-called ideals of "liberty" and "justice" and "indivisibility" are simply PR myths we like to trumpet and parade around for the sake of appearances. When it comes to truly establishing and maintaining such aims, we fall woefully short.

But we could fix a lot of this mess by revising the last line of the pledge. If it read "one heterosexual nation, under God, with liberty and justice for all straight people," it would obviously allow us to seem less counterfeit.

A gay family friend of mine serves in the U.S. Military. I often wonder how he feels risking his life, serving his country, knowing that his neighbors back home shun him—but doing his duty anyway.

Could there be any better way to demonstrate our appreciation for his service than granting him the same rights and privileges that all Americans are supposed to enjoy? Why should he be asked to fight for ideals that don't apply to him? Why does he put his life on the line for a bunch of hypocrites?

The U.S. Military's current policy on homosexuality is "Don't ask, don't tell." If it isn't brought up, the brass doesn't have to address it.

Perhaps the same principle should be exercised regarding the pledge. It we don't recite this flawed oath, then we don't have to delude ourselves or lie to the victims of our charade.

Eye of the Codger
Dissident Voice • June 4, 2007

Years ago, during a college graduation commencement address, Sylvester Stallone instructed graduates to lie on their resumés.

To be fair, he probably made the suggestion half-jokingly, but also, perhaps, in an effort to level with them about how hard it can be to get your foot in the door. One of Stallone's first pictures was a porno. Like most old hands in Hollywood, he knew you had to be ready to do whatever it took and, if necessary, cut corners. Needless to say, his advice wasn't well-received.

I remembered this obscure trivia when I heard that Stallone had gotten busted for mistakenly smuggling human growth hormone into Australia earlier this month. He was apparently on his way to Southeast Asia to film the latest installment of *Rambo*.

Still cutting corners, I guess. But prepared to do whatever it takes.

As a fading, but still almost universally recognizable Hollywood icon, there is no doubt Stallone figured his baggage would receive less scrutiny than most travelers' and this assumption got him into a bit of a pickle. But if *Rambo IV* is at least a moderate box office hit, the pickle will serve as little more than the relish that we put on our hot dogs when we cram into megaplex theatres to watch Stallone gratuitously beat the stuffing out of foreign evildoers in some quasi-noble cause Americana.

Rambo's brand of justice will no doubt be the product of performance-enhancing human growth hormones, but we won't give it a second thought because, like diehard baseball fans, we don't care what our heroes are hopped up on as long as they are kicking ass.

Therein arguably lies the biggest downside of being a screen idol. No one wants to see you grow old and, when you do, you lose appeal, garner less attention and demand and, ultimately, become passé. The celebrity and adulation you enjoyed as a star begins to fade and soon you're just a cinematic footnote.

Marilyn Monroe and James Dean got off easy. They died relatively young and before their appearance and screen appeal had begun to seriously deteriorate. Bogart had begun to fade, but passed away before a complete aesthetic collapse. Brando held up well through *The Godfather*, but started gaining weight by *Apocalypse Now* and never slimmed back down. He went the way of Orson Welles, but at least never had to resort to wine commercials.

The chief male Hollywood icon that comes to mind as having aged with style and grace is Paul Newman. He's eighty-two this year. He never gained much weight, never pumped himself up to stave off wrinkles and never injected synthetic hormones to beef up his screen appeal. He seemed to take advancing years as they came, maturing, growing—allowing himself to age and act his age. Stallone obviously isn't following in his footsteps.

A screen icon like Stallone—even with all his insanely popular hits in the 80s—is no heavyweight like Brando or Newman. Or even Dean. But his films did titillate the American psyche for a time. In the original *Rocky*, Stallone rewrote Brando's "Terry Malloy," from *On the Waterfront*, allowing him not to become just a contender, but a champion. And in the original *Rambo*, Stallone puts a twist on Robert DeNiro's "Michael Vronsky," from *The Deer Hunter*. In an exaggerated meditation on being a discarded vet of an unpopular war, Stallone's "Rambo" externalizes his frustrations and indignation towards the society that under-appreciates him, and terrorizes a small town full of yokels.

The film was hokey, but still a huge success. And *Rambo II* succeeded even further, stoking patriotic disdain for the purported political bureaucracy that prevented us from "winning" the Vietnam War and, more importantly, giving Ronnie Reagan unlimited mileage in his Cold War meanderings by depicting Rambo as a righteous American warrior doing battle with evil cardboard cut-out Communist (Vietnamese, Russian, etc.) villains (Thank god George W. Bush didn't have an ass-kicking, put-upon ideologue like John Rambo taking it to the Islamic Extremists on the silver screen during the first few years of our "war" in Iraq — his approval rating would still be over 50%!?!).

I'm sure *Rambo IV* will be at least mildly entertaining to the multitude, because Stallone is still clever enough to milk his most iconoclastic characters for likable, low-brow epilogues. But behind the nostalgic, feel-good revue is the ugly downside of life.

We get old. We don't look as good. We don't get around as well. It's unpleasant and frustrating, but also natural and authentic. The real deal.

Watching sixty-year-olds like Stallone stomp around in artificially enhanced muscles isn't terribly inspirational. It's fake, it's silly and it's sad. I have no problem with raging against the dying of the light, but there's a big difference between standing up and leaning into the wind with what's left of your natural fortitude or dignity and injecting synthetic napalm into your bloodstream so you can storm the box office for one or two final, frenzied flameouts before you collapse.

I'd rather remember Stallone the way he was depicted in the original *Rocky* or the recent *Copland* (in which he still looked like a normal human being), instead of *Rocky VI* or *Rambo IV*.

Did he need the money? Did he just want his two most successful silver screen characters to go out in a decent production rather than the drivel they had succumbed to in the late 80s? Neither reason makes shooting up with human growth hormone worth the price of admission.

In *Cobra*, "Marion Cobretti," one of Stallone's most forgettable characters, calls a dangerous thug a "disease" to which he—Cobra—is the "cure." These days, respectable sequels, favorable reviews and/or box office successes or no, Stallone is part of the disease. The cure is box office absenteeism.

Ultimate Reality Check

Fort Worth Star-Telegram • *December 21, 2009*

Suicide is a touchy subject during the holidays. Lots of folks consider it, and too many people commit it. It's a disturbing yuletide paradox.

Nobel Prize Laureate Albert Camus once suggested that the most important question philosophy could answer is whether or not we should kill ourselves. It's an astonishing remark that's easy to dismiss, especially if we approach it abruptly. It's blasphemous. It cuts to the quick. It's such a provocative statement that it seems like an attack; but it's not. It's simply an existential reality check.

In the grand scheme of things, we may be specks of dust gravitationally attached to a spinning pebble that's flying thru the universe at approximately 16,000 mph, surrounded by billions of other speeding, spinning pebbles powdered with trillions of other specks of dust. And our smallish, brief existences are regimented by petty, spirit-crushing vocational requirements, ludicrous societal institutions and frivolous material wants.

Instead of living, we are preoccupied with "making" a living. Instead of making sure we have what we need, we obsess over getting what we want. Instead of being ourselves, we trudge through our days simply being who we're expected to be.

Camus pointed to the absurdities of modern culture and simply asked whether life was worth living if we had to reduce ourselves to such inanity. He posited that once choosing between life and death became a matter of principle, we were compelled to make a choice.

Obviously, most of us weigh in affirmatively, easily finding ways to justify our lives. Many rationales are shallow and contrived, but they're safe and sustainable and they allow us to function as conventionally productive individuals.

On an individual level, then, our answer to Camus' question is a resounding "Life *is* worth living." We teach it, we preach it and we cling to it. We live our lives as if there's more to us than meets the eye, as if there's a reason we're here, as if we have something indispensable to contribute. We affirm our existences every day, from the minute we get out of bed to the moment we fall asleep.

Unfortunately, as we individually proclaim that life is worth living, we collectively indicate otherwise.

As a species, we conduct ourselves as if life were not worth living, much less preserving. We live irresponsibly and self-destructively, as if our actions (and/or inaction) had no consequences.

We poison and pollute our natural habitat for the sake of mass production and steeper profit margins. We squander our natural resources to maintain cultures of indulgence and material extravagance. We base our politics on greed and entitlement. We base our economics on carbon-based fuels and war-mongering. We mortgage our future well-being for instant gratification, short-term gains and incessant modes of entertainment, leisure and general escapism.

Surely, if we found life worth living, we'd be interested in conserving and protecting our natural resources for future generations. We wouldn't allow our political representatives to trivialize climate concerns, block emission reductions or depreciate renewable energy sources. We'd be more committed to addressing ozone depletion, oceanic dead zones, deforestation, desertification, extreme weather events, bee colony collapse disorder, animal and plant extinctions, and the rest of the readily identifiable messes we are collectively responsible for.

Cosmologically speaking, we may be specks of dust on this planet, but our actions have consequences and our existences leave imprints. Isn't it time we started considering the consequences of living unsustainably? *Isn't it time we stopped leaving a suicidal imprint?*

New Year's Eve is just around the corner. Our resolution needs to be a profound one.

We Can Move the Earth

Fort Worth Weekly • *November 9, 2011*

On Feb. 8, 2008, I felt the earth move beneath my feet. It wasn't an earthquake or a Hemingway-esque tryst. It was simply a gathering of dendraster excentricus, otherwise known as Pacific sand dollars.

The few times I got to visit the beach while I was growing up, I loved finding sand dollars. But I never quite grasped that they had actually been alive. Even though every seashell once housed a living creature, it was hard to think of the thin, bleached disks that way.

I still carried this misconception when I stepped onto a Pacific beach in Nicaragua in 2008. My wife and I were walking along the water's edge and I stepped just deep enough into the waves to get our ankles wet. As the surf came and went, I felt the sand shift under one foot and then the other. A little spooked, I high-stepped up to dry land as fast as I could. What had I stepped on? My limited experience with the ocean hadn't included this.

I later found out that I had walked over a swarm of sand dollars. They were alive and burrowing into the sand, using the thousands of tiny velvety spines that covered their surfaces. The ones that beachcombers collected in the mornings were actually dead sand dollars that got washed up too far on dry land and couldn't make it back to the surf. Their velvety outer layer had fallen away, and they had skeletonized in the sun.

That memory has come back to me vividly in recent weeks because of the Occupy movements around the country.

The earth is moving under our feet. The young and the young-at-heart are writhing and twisting and jerking beneath the weight of cataclysmic economic powers and rejecting the heretofore unassailable status quo.

Like so many of the rest of you, I'm something of a bleached white corpse. I washed up too far on the beach long ago and lost the way or the energy to regain the surf. But these Occupy folks are still alive, still breathing and moving, hoping and dreaming, still acting as if they might be able to change some things.

Why aren't you and I there with them?

Is it too late for us?

I follow their progress every night. I marvel at their ingenuity. I am humbled by their courage. I am proud of their passion.

Sure, there are some clowns in the crowd, but the core is informed, disciplined, and solid—as good as we could ever aspire to be.

In the '60s, a lot of folks rejected the hippies, for their appearances and their clear threat to authority as much as for their ideology. But the funny thing is that so many of the ideas that the counterculture worked and stood for back then—a freer sexual climate, environmental awareness, racial and gender equality—have become part of the accepted fabric of our country. And all these decades later, many of those who were the most virulently opposed to those long-haired, free-lovin', peace-seeking masses of young people have looked back and discovered they were on the wrong side of history.

The same thing will happen here. The Occupy movement is on the right side of history. The young and the young-at-heart are pointing us in the right direction. The powers that be—economic and otherwise—have treated us and the system in which we operate like throw rugs. The powers that be have been stupid and greedy, and everyone knows it. And now those of us with fight left in our craws or courage left in our hearts are occupying, mobilizing, marching, and protesting. It's as exciting a human moment as most of us will ever witness.

This is no time to admire the spectacle from afar or gaze longingly from the sidelines. History is being made, and our democracy is being refined. These Occupations are the best of us and the best of what's left, after decades of having been whittled down by banal materialism, existential impotence, and the resultant dreary resignation.

It's not too late, even for human varieties of washed-up *dendraster excentricus*. Our voices can become one voice. We can make the earth move.

Will They Eventually
Stomp Some "Sense" into Us?
Unpublished • August 2012

When 17th century philosopher Baruch Spinoza was eight years-old, he witnessed members of his synagogue trampling a man. When he precociously asked them what they were doing, they said the man beneath their heels was a free thinker and they were simply stomping the sins out of him.

These days spiritual and philosophical conservatives don't have to resort to trampling. Independent thought is a giant social and metaphysical pickle, but conservatives' methods—unlike their core belief systems—have evolved.

Many conservatives still smother their offspring with anti-quated moral absolutism, staid instructions for righteousness and a general environment of stale-mindedness. And most conserva-tives still openly discourage intellectual curiosity and broad spiri-tual survey—but now they're more realistic about it. They realize a tedious regimen of planned ignorance invites serious, short-term repercussions like young (and bright) people leaving the cause or church; but they've come to terms with the often unpal-atable nature of their spiritual screed because studies show that human beings almost invariably revert back to their initial default settings, no matter what they see or do or experience in the inter-im between their original inculcation and their almost involuntary return to the fold.

So conservatives are now more focused on their long game.

Get 'em while they're young, mostly intellectually defenseless and predominantly vulnerable to indoctrination. Lay the message on thick and repeat it incessantly. Even if good sheep are away for years or stray for decades after their original indoctrination, most return to what they were taught to believe and think before they had a choice. The process has done wonders for racism, sexism, extremism and religion for centuries (if not millennia). And it's still at work today.

To make sure little is left to chance, contemporary conservatives are doubling down, fortifying their leanings with additional mechanisms to curb free thought.

First, they discourage it in the very institutions created to encourage it. Consider the Republican Party in Texas. In its 2012 platform, it openly opposes the cultivation of high order thinking skills, critical reasoning and similar advanced cognitive processes in our schools because they might challenge a students fixed beliefs and undermine parental authority. Translation: They don't want folks thinking for themselves—they simply want us to accept and do what we're told.

Don't laugh … it's working. We've had a haircut for a governor for twelve years and he won the last gubernatorial race without even engaging in a debate. We're not thinking, much less thinking for ourselves, and that's exactly what's expected of us.

Second, conservatives have established 24/7 propaganda machines that selectively interpret the news and disinclude mention, coverage and honest analysis of any events or developments that occur or trend contrariwise to their worldview. Fox News is the best example, but fear- and hatemongers like Rush Limbaugh and Glenn Beck (now comfortably based in our back yard) are concurrent conservative institutions in their own right. The paranoid, quasi-rational xenophobes created by regressive implantation now have prominent airwave and broadcast outlets to daily affirm their prejudices, bigotry and superstition so they can remain little or ill-informed in sheltered peace.

There's a dangerous, unapproachable mob of these folks marching lock-step around the country now, growling and snarling, nodding in dim agreement, eyeing progressives, free spirits, immigrants and eggheads and wondering why more isn't being done about them and to them.

Fox News, Limbaugh, Beck, et al are sustaining and creating more of this mob and the current conservative end game teases being something like a dozen angry feebs following Sarah Palin door-to-door with torches and pitchforks in hand and a guillotine or dunking stool secured to the trailer behind her Range Rover.

It's funny, but it's not.

It's preposterous—but it's also scary.

The new conservative litmus test runs the gamut on "backwards."

Climate change is a hoax, carbon dating is a hoax, evolutionary theory is a con, the Earth is only 7,000 years-old, modern humans rode dinosaurs, torture is necessary and President Obama is a Manchurian Kenyan who hates America and white people—including his mother. Just ask Glenn Beck.

Of all the tipping points humanity flirts with, I submit that the most dangerous and disheartening are the increasing instances and apparent success of willful imbecility in United States as a whole and as a troubling force in the world. As long as Right-wing barkers continue to make fortunes encouraging indoctrinated conservative reactionaries to take their country back from black presidents, open-minded young people and the dwindling secular forces of compassion and conscience (that conservatives are conditioned to despise), the ideals that America was meant to represent will continue to be trampled on. And if some sense isn't injected into the conservative conversation soon, conservatives may eventually stomp some senselessness into all of us.

If a 50-foot Woman Falls Dead and
No One Notices, Does She Make a Sound?
Dissident Voice • *May 18, 2011*

On April 27th, Yvette Vickers, an eighty-two-year-old former *Playboy* playmate and star of *Attack of the 50 Foot Woman*, was found dead in her Los Angeles home. Her remains were mummified and she'd been deceased for several months. Her fame and beauty were long gone and she passed away in solitary anonymity.

On February 18th, a fifty-one-year-old L.A. County auditor named Rebecca Wells died in a cubicle at the California Department of Internal Services. Her demise wasn't discovered until the following afternoon. No one approached her upright corpse until a relative called to report her missing.

In January 2009, Nebraska resident Mary Sue Merchant neglected to pay $234 in property taxes. The county she lived in sent a delinquency letter to her post office box, but it was returned because she never responded. On December 1, 2010, the county sold her $160,000 home (complete with a recent model four-door Chevy out front) for $20,000. When someone finally examined the property, they discovered Merchant's dead body in the house with her dead dog nearby. Merchant had died of natural causes almost two years prior. Her dog had died of thirst shortly thereafter.

In early 2006, Long Island resident Vicenzo Ricardo sat down on his couch and turned on his television. Unlike his 200 million fellow American TV consumers however, Ricardo didn't turn the TV off that evening or the next evening or the evening after that. Ricardo sat on his couch in front of the television for a year straight. His TV didn't get turned off until mid-February of 2007, when a group of workers were dispatched to his address because freezing weather had caused his water pipes to burst.

Inside the workers found his well-preserved, mummified remains still propped up in TV-viewing repose. His power had never been cut off.

For the first half of the 20th century, your average American knew their butcher, milkman, grocer, paper boy, banker, neighbors, etc. Their relationships weren't virtual and their conversations weren't electronic. They didn't have each other at the push of a button that could just as easily have raised someone else at a different push of a button. They knew each other; they depended on each other. They were connected.

Now, we're simply linked.

And because of our lack of real human connections and dwindling, practical, face-to-face interpersonal relationships, too many of us live and die in unacknowledged isolation.

Metaphysically speaking, an unobserved event—like the deaths of Vickers, Wells, Merchant and Ricardo—has no perceivable effect, so an unobserved incident is identical to a non-event. If Vickers' neighbor hadn't decided to check on her, she'd still be mummifying. If Merchant's house hadn't have been sold out from underneath her, she and her dog would still be lying in the dark. If Ricardo's water pipes hadn't burst, his TV might still be on as if he was still alive and soaking up the deceitful selling points and clever ad copy that shape the glittering unreality that thrives due to our disconnectedness.

Sometimes people just fall through the cracks. Sometimes it's isolated individuals; sometimes it's whole social and economic classes. The wealthy elites who run our country obviously don't hear us falling. They're so insulated from our struggles that our collapse has mostly been a non-event.

I fear in the end the stories of Vickers, Wells, Merchant and Ricardo will be our stories and humanity's story. Eventually, there will be a virus or super-bacteria or bomb or cataclysmic cosmic or climate event. We'll die in front of our TVs or in cubicles or in traffic and no one will notice.

The machines that we've left on will eventually shut off. The mythologies we fought over will become little more than oily films on the surface of the ocean.

Nature's observance of our passing will only be acknowledged in its sudden thrivings, its new abundances and the re-enfranchisement of its *natural* law-abiding citizens.

Yvette Vickers, Rebecca Wells, Mary Sue Merchant, and Vincenzo Ricardo are forebodings of what we as a culture and a species are dithering toward.

Republicans and Their Guns

Dissident Voice • January 12, 2011

Republicans can disavow responsibility for Jared Loughner all they want, but he was wearing Christine O'Donnell's "man-pants," he did exercise Susan Angle's interpretation of the 2nd Amendment, and he did use conservative radio host Joyce Kaufman's bullets when the ballots didn't work. Oh, and he did get a Democrat in Sarah Palin's bull's eye crosshairs.

Most folks are tiptoeing around the partisan nature of the shooting of U.S. Congresswoman Gabrielle Giffords and others in Tucson, but count me among the uncouth. There is blood on conservative hands and they should be called out. Another homicidal nut-job has brought their irresponsible rhetoric to fruition and they should answer for it.

I don't want to hear Republicans saying there's no place for this kind of violence in this country or condemning Loughner as an isolated, incidental mad man. Especially as if it's something new or unexpected. Conservative rhetoric has been cranked up way past the "stun" setting ever since the Bush Administration was on its last crooked leg. And the target audience for their hate-speak has clearly been compelled.

Lest we forget, it was a conservative who walked into his former church in Knoxville, Tennessee on July 28, 2008 and shot eight people (killing two) because liberals "were ruining the country" (and his church had gotten too liberal). It was conservatives who were brandishing firearms at political events in the 2008 presidential campaign. It was a conservative evangelical Christian who shot abortion doctor George Tiller at his church in Kansas on May 31, 2009. It was a conservative white supremacist who shot security guard Stephen Tyrone Johns at the Holocaust Museum on June 10, 2009. And it was arguably an anti-government conservative that flew his plane into the IRS office in Austin, Texas on February 10, 2010.

There is no reason to mince words.

Violence is implicit in conservative rhetoric because its audience honestly believes dissenters should be vilified and punished, and it thrills the Republicans' conservative base to see its philosophical opponents squirm. Threatening language is necessary for their cause because fear and hatred are presently the load-bearing joists in their political platform. And what's more, deep down, they're not even ashamed of it.

Rush Limbaugh once blamed John Edwards' affair with Rielle Hunter on Elizabeth Edwards, now deceased. He said that John Edwards sought companionship with Hunter because, unlike his wife, Rielle "did something with her mouth other than talk." It was callous and repugnant, but it wasn't scripted, and it didn't diminish Limbaugh's ratings one iota. The comment was telling about who Limbaugh is and how he thinks, but also about who his audience is and how they think. The truth is, it's not hard to imagine Limbaugh serving up something equally asinine about Congresswoman Giffords. Right now, he wouldn't dare because there's too much heat. But just because he isn't saying it doesn't mean he's not thinking it.

And this is why Limbaugh is the voice for so many conservatives in this country. He touches a nerve with his listeners; he teases a brutish, authoritarian strain in them that reveres clichés like "my country right or wrong," " love it or leave it," etc. And these folks take comfort in implied threats for people who disagree with them. That's why they can rationalize the notion that the ends justify the means.

Deep down, they're not really bothered by the combustible letter that was sent to Janet Napolitano; she's from the wrong side of the aisle. And somewhere inside they're not terribly upset by what happened to Giffords, because she's the ideological enemy. They can't help themselves. It's just who they are.

But one of these days a sharp contrarian will finally expose it. It will be like the showdown scene from *A Few Good Men*. The contrarian will get a Limbaugh or a Beck or a Palin or an Allen West on a "stand" and challenge their methods and their authority and their warped world view and badger them and demand the truth; and that Limbaugh, Beck, Palin or West will say the rest of us can't handle the truth and launch into a blustery diatribe explaining that heathens like Tiller and liberals like Giffords got what they had coming to them and the country is a better place with every less one of them around.

And everyone will be shocked and offended except those in gun-toting red states who, deep down, can see what Limbaugh, Beck, Palin and West were really trying to say, before they were misquoted or misinterpreted.

Wanted: Poets

Fort Worth Weekly • *March 14, 2012*

Writer Don DeLillo once wrote that reading poetry makes us conscious of breathing. I can't imagine a better way to put it.

The first time I fell in love, really fell in love, it was not with a girl or a woman. It was with a smattering of words here and there on a page. A printed page.

It presaged what love would be like.

It said *love is a jigsaw sunset and you are the peace that holds the sun.*

It said *the best gesture of my brain is less than the flutter of your eyelids which whisper we are made for each other.*

It took my breath away and then gave it back, deeper and more meaningful. I wanted to take in as much of it as I could.

While other kids were dreaming about throwing or catching the winning touchdown pass or chasing after the boy who threw or caught the winning touchdown pass, I discovered trunkless legs of stone in a faraway desert, wandered the stately pleasure-dome of Kubla Khan and pondered fears of what would happen if I ceased to be. My eyes widened and the narrows of obviousness rapidly became too confining.

I never idolized Luke Skywalker or Dr. J.

I wanted to be Poe. I wanted to be Keats or Shelley or Yeats. I wanted to speak to people in a way that made them conscious of breathing.

Today air intake is just an involuntary reflex. Consciousness of it is something we attempt to force on our kids in school or college, but it doesn't stick. And perhaps it was always so.

It's been over two hundred years since Wordsworth noted that devoting our lives to getting and spending lays waste to our spirits. And we're still mostly just getting and spending.

There's not a business department in the land that will tell you that breathing is more important than getting and spending. Especially someone else's breathing.

Society pays no praise or wages for the sullen art I loved because it taught me to love and breathe lovingly. And I know I have become a boring anachronism.

But I feel compelled to resist. I fear the reduction of our culture to raps and tweets and texts. The ironic truth about I-Touches, I-Pads and I-Phones is that more people are communicating, but less is being said. The gadgets truncate our thought processes and abridge cognition. They comprise a strain of expedience that might be useful in an immediate sense, but will likely be detrimental in the longer sense.

This is no time for intellectual slang. Look around.

The ceremony of innocence is being drowned. The best lack conviction and *the worst are full of passionate intensity.*

The mob may be incited or mollified by a text or tweet, but it will not be moved in a meaningful direction. That requires elucidation and crafted cogence.

Shelley may have overshot the mark when he said that poets are the unacknowledged legislators of the world, but even if it isn't true, it should be.

The world is so much with us that we fail to grasp the importance of the moment we live in and exist oblivious to the repercussions.

We need to be more conscious of our breathing.

We must become more mindful of our interconnectedness with everything and everyone around us. There's no hope for us as a single party, cause, country, religion, ethnicity or species. Our only hope lies in collective conscience and broad concert.

Instead of getting and spending we need to do more watching and listening and thinking.

Instead of ceding conviction to brainwashed miscreants and manipulative scoundrels, we need to speak out and rise up, inspired and informed, and therefore indomitable.

We don't need more pundits or politicians or profiteers. We don't need unlimited texts or more folks following us on Twitter.

We need more eloquence and profundity.

We need more poets.

Reality Bites

Fort Worth Weekly • *May 3, 2006*

I have a six-year-old son. A couple of weeks ago, he got spooked while we were watching *The Day After Tomorrow*. In fact, during the scene that depicted the tornados in Los Angeles, he ran out of the living room and hid.

He returned shortly, after peeking around the corner to make sure the tornadoes were gone. He sat down next to me on the couch and stayed close. Then, he looked up at me and said "Is it real, Daddy?"

I paused the movie and put my arms around him.

"No," I said. "It's not real. It's just a movie."

It was a pat answer. Something we've all said to our kids. I didn't think much of it at first, but I woke up in the middle of the night and couldn't get it out of my mind. I realized I had lied.

It wasn't a lie of commission but one of omission. The stuff in *The Day After Tomorrow* isn't real—yet. But it's coming. I left that part out.

Scenarios like the ones featured in *The Day After Tomorrow* are coming, and maybe even in his lifetime. Global warming is changing worldwide weather patterns, and mounting evidence suggests that there'll be more hurricanes, flooding, and tornadoes. And they'll be stronger and more destructive.

Last month, *Science* magazine reported on research indicating that ocean levels may rise as much as three feet by the year 2100, as polar ice begins to melt due to increasing Earth temperatures. That means New Orleans and Miami will be under water. That means relocating New Orleans would be a better idea than rebuilding it. That means the beaches here in Texas may get a lot closer to the

Metroplex.

Just three days prior to that, the United Nations also released a report stating that our species has now achieved the distinction of serving as the chief catalyst for the worst catalog of global extinctions since the dinosaurs disappeared 65 million years ago. There are now 6.5 billion of us, and we're destroying every habitat we inhabit at a breakneck pace through overpopulation, exploitation, air pollution, water pollution, deforestation, global warming, etc.

We like to think it's not happening here, but when is the last time you saw a horny toad? When I was growing up, they were all over the place. The Fort Worth area was one of their natural habitats. Now, except as a mascot for TCU, they're gone.

Will I live long enough to be forced to apologize to my son for lying? Will I live long enough to share in the hell he and his children are going to inherit?

The times we live in are characterized by a ferocious will to ignorance. We detest bad news. We don't trust our politicians. We despise the media for not telling us what we want to hear. We just want to watch *American Idol*. And shop. And play fantasy football and golf. And listen to our iPods. And let someone else worry about the consequences.

We want the future to be as far away for us as it was for our parents. We desperately want to think highly of ourselves and be happy with the status quo. We want a life without consequences.

This isn't going to be possible.

Somewhere down the line someone will have to pay for our complacence, our lack of discipline, our total disregard for the repercussions of our lack of conscience and fortitude. That someone will likely be my son or my son's son. They'll pay for our sins.

I am haunted by my son's question. We're consuming ourselves into oblivion. Hamlet's "quintessence of dust" has emerged to be a quintessential leveler. The meek are not inheriting the earth so much as destroying it.

Is it real?

Fifteen years ago the famous French ecologist Jacques Cousteau said that we were turning more and more toward "needless consumption" and that our species' only hope might be the diseases or plagues that could curb the destructive trend of human overpopulation.

Is it real?

Earlier this year, world-renowned British scientist James Lovelock predicted that we've already passed the point of no return and that before this century ends, billions will die and the few surviving human breeding pairs will flee to the Arctic—the only place the climate will remain tolerable.

Is it real?

It's real every time we start at the sports pages instead of the news sections in the newspaper. It's real every time we elect narrow-minded simpletons who deny that global warming exists. It's real every day we continue to let multi-national corporations increase their profit margins at the expense of the planet and its people. It's real every time we go to the gas pump. It's real every minute of every hour of every day that you and I continue to just hope things won't get any worse instead of taking responsibility for the impending problems and committing ourselves to remedial action.

Is it real?

Yes. If it wasn't real, I wouldn't have to lie to my son.

The Recent Facts Regarding a Capitalist Crime in Cowtown

Dissident Voice • *April 14, 2011*

It's hard for me to pick a favorite spot in Fort Worth. I dig every nook and cranny of The Modern. I like the Water Gardens. I love the four leaning, tornado-twisted steel girders at the Museum Place Post Office. But perhaps the spot dearest to my heart is sitting next to Mark Twain in Trinity Park.

He sits in bronzed repose on a park bench on the westerly side of the Trinity River, thumbing through a copy of *The Adventures of Huckleberry Finn*. Why he's depicted reading his own book, I don't know. It's probably just an over-conspicuous hint for scantily literate folks who pass by. Regardless, what I cherish about Twain's presence at this specific geographic location is the simple irony of it.

Early in 1873, the *New York Tribune* asked Mark Twain what he thought about the annexation of Hawaii. In the January 9 edition, Twain wrote "We must annex these people," sarcastically noting that we can give them "juries comprised of idiots," introduce corporations that will "buy their legislatures like old clothes" and furnish them with Capitalists "who will do away with their old-time notions that stealing is not respectable."

Hawaii didn't get annexed for another eighty-six years, but Twain's satirical commentary was spot on then and is still spot on today.

Ill-informed by perfidious cable news channels and talk-radio cranks, we have become a nation of morons, that is hardly capable of sober jurisprudence and increasingly undeserving of democracy. Corporations openly buy and sell our political representatives and unabashedly manipulate them through expensive political groupies (better known as lobbyists). And Capitalists—well, they obviously care more about making money than anything else, "dishonestly if they can and honestly if they must" (as Twain himself noted in the "The Revised Catechism").

The Golden Rule is no longer "Do unto others as you would have them do unto you." It's *Do unto others before they do unto you* or *Do unto others in ways that will benefit you*. Ethics are for suckers and morals are for the poor (or what in the 21st century refer to as the Middle Class).

Twain saw all this 138 years ago and wasn't shy about calling folks out. And that's why it's ironic that he sits where he sits in Trinity Park.

You see, the east side of the Trinity River where Twain sits is the south-westernmost edge of the 76102 zip code; the 76102 zip code of downtown Fort Worth leads the entire nation in political contributions made by the oil and gas industry. There are a staggering 43,000 zip codes in the United States, and our bronzed Twain sits facing the boundary of one of the zip codes that most profoundly evidences the type of ridiculous status quo that he sarcastically insisted we should impose on the Hawaiians.

The oil and gas outfits in the 76102 have spent millions on local and national political hides and that's why they get away with transforming kitchen sinks into flamethrowers, polluting our water supplies, fouling the air we breathe and "fracking" the ground beneath us so much that it's actually causing minor earthquakes and tremors.

We have no idea or understanding of what the long-term effects of environmental and seismic onslaughts of this magnitude will lead to, but the short-term economic benefits of the local natural gas boom keep us agreeable to being *done unto* and dumb to the possible catastrophic future repercussions. In matters regarding the Barnett Shale, our politicians take care of their corporate patrons and we're little more than collateral victims in a dangerous experiment in old-time Capitalism.

Twain would have viewed the oil and gas industries the same

way he viewed the railroad corporations in the last part of the 19th century: treacherous, short-sighted miscreants who have no qualms about ignoring, going around or running over a community or its watchful citizens if they get between them and higher profit margins. And that's what's happened to us; we've been *done unto* in underhanded, cold-blooded ways that most of us don't even begin to understand.

That's why a seat next to Twain is my favorite spot in Fort Worth. Even though his mustachioed headpiece is made of hollow bronze, he's still got more sense than too many of us.

Force to Live

Fort Worth Weekly • *February 8, 2006*

On August 1, 1966, David H. Gunby was a twenty-three-year-old engineering student at the University of Texas. After a round of studying at a campus library, he walked out into the courtyard of the UT Tower. As he crossed the courtyard, he became one of Charles Whitman's first victims. Whitman shot him in the lower left side of his back.

As he lay on the ground wounded, he could see Whitman up in the tower. When other students attempted to run out and help him, Gunby waved them off. He knew Whitman would fire at anyone else who appeared out in the open.

By the end of the day, seventeen people (including Whitman) were dead or dying, and thirty-three were wounded. When Gunby finally made it to the hospital, doctors found that Whitman's bullet had severed his small intestine. As doctors performed surgery to repair the intestine, they also discovered that Gunby had only one kidney and that it, too, had been damaged by bullet fragments.

According to published reports, Gunby never fully recovered. After the shooting, he suffered repeated kidney problems and eventually received a kidney transplant. His body rejected the new kidney, and he almost died.

Gunby finished his degree and settled here in Fort Worth. He raised two children with his wife and worked at General Dynamics. For the last twenty-seven years of his life, Gunby endured kidney dialysis three times a week. He was in constant pain, but that didn't stop him from being a good provider, father, and husband.

On November 7, 2001, Gunby decided to stop dialysis. He was

pronounced dead at Harris Methodist Hospital a week later. He was Whitman's 18th victim.

There's no way anyone who knew David Gunby or carefully read the preceding passages about him could consider him anything less than a courageous man. Life dealt him a tragic hand, and he did the best he could. And when he finally wore down and didn't want to subject himself to the constant physical infirmity any longer, he arranged to end his life.

To social and religious conservatives, what Gunby did was a sin. They believe that only their God should have control or authority over whether we live or die. Last month, the U.S. Supreme Court disagreed with them.

In a 6-3 decision, the high court rejected the Bush administration's challenge to Oregon's "right-to-die" law and ruled that former U.S. Attorney General John Ashcroft had overstepped his authority when he tried to punish Oregon doctors for assisting terminally ill persons in their efforts to end their own lives. The decision came not long after intervention by the Republican-led Congress in the Terri Schiavo case last year, which also resulted in an ideological setback for social conservatives when the Supreme Court balked on taking up the case.

Apparently, conservative stalwarts just don't get the point. Suffering folks like David Gunby are peacefully abridging their existences without God's permission, and the "force-to-live" faction, as I like to call them, just can't allow them that right.

If the religious right really has absolute faith in God's control over human life and death, why don't they skip the pleasantries and lobby to abolish doctors and medicine altogether? If God has decided it's our time to go, wouldn't a doctor simply be interfering in God's plan? Was it God's plan for Charles Whitman to blow a hole in David Gunby's back? Was it God's plan for Gunby to spend the last twenty-seven years of his life enduring the hell of kidney dialysis three times a week? If you were David Gunby, wouldn't you have had enough of God's plan? Could anyone honestly blame him for taking matters into his own hands?

Why do Christians have such a problem with suicide? Jesus

Christ was a great guy, and the accounts we have of his existence certainly make it worth emulating. But the lives of lots of people and prophets are worth emulating. What made the early Jewish religion different from many other belief systems of the time was its constituents' refusal to compromise their existence by abandoning their beliefs. The Jews at Masada chose to hurl themselves over the cliff rather than proclaim the Roman emperor their god—down to the last woman and child. They decided to commit suicide rather than abdicate their religious faith. In the end, such devotion and fidelity overcame even the Romans. They couldn't strong-arm a people who opted for death over compromised life. What was David Gunby's life if not physically compromised?

The term "liberty" in the phrase "life, liberty, and the pursuit of happiness" is not the property of self-righteous religious groups. It's the established right of every individual American. One of the great things about America is that no one can tell you how to live your life. In that case, why should anyone be allowed to tell you how you can end it?

The recent attempts by the Republican Party's "force-to-live" faction to usurp and restrict existential freedoms should be met with defiance and scorn. Who are they to decide whether someone like David Gunby had suffered enough?

Whistling Dixie

Fort Worth Weekly • *August 20, 2014*

This is a strange time in American history. I don't recognize us.

And by us, I mean white people.

We seethe with hatred. We're fed up and embittered. Things aren't going our way, and somebody needs to pay. Someone deserves blame.

Our better angels have flown the coop, and our inner demons are ruling the roost. On a daily basis, whole legions of us prostrate ourselves before hateful messiahs who spray inane vitriol, and we clamor for more.

I'm not convinced that it's even happening on a conscious level. For millions of Americans, I fear, this has become a reflex, conditioned by incessant guilt and self-loathing.

The history of slavery in this country is reprehensible. It was an unconscionable monstrosity. We don't like to think about the reality of it, the depravity that allowed it to flourish, or the fact that half the country was willing to die to defend it. Here in Texas we even threw over our own George Washington—Sam Houston himself—after he refused to lead us gently into that "good" Confederacy, which he saw as a horrific mistake. Two dozen Texas counties and thousands of sober folks sided with Houston, but he lost. Houston's woeful banishment and Texas' subsequent descent into the Civil War are hardly taught in our history books, much less touched on in serious conversation.

A century and a half has gone by, and we like to think (rather wishfully) that all is forgotten or can be forgotten. We insist it's time to move on, but we want to do so without ever having truly examined our slave-owning past.

Electing a black president made us feel a little better until we realized we had actually elected a black president. A representative of the victims of our vilest monstrosity had risen to the highest office in the land, the most powerful job in the world. While we were busy proclaiming racism dead, this young, black Gen-X president was a constant reminder of what we had labored tirelessly to forget. And he was tasked with attempting to lead us through a perilous patch, fraught with dangers domestic, foreign and economic.

When the opposition party decided to make the race card part of its political platform, it quickly legitimized our conscious and unconscious unease with the memories that Barack Obama nudged us to confront. This unease helped promote Obama's vilification and encouraged us to feel nostalgic for (or at least more comfortable with) the good ol' days when our past wasn't considered a monstrosity and racial prejudice was a point of pride.

History will judge our current lapse unmercifully.

Our internal and often external backlash to Barrack Obama's presidency is beginning to manifest itself in shocking ways. If we didn't have a black president, we wouldn't be vowing to "take our country back." If we didn't have a black president, we wouldn't be showing up at town halls and Home Depots with guns (as if we were about to try and take our country back). If our president wasn't black, George Zimmerman would have been held accountable for the murder of Trayvon Martin.

And, I fear, if the leader of the "free" world wasn't a black man, unarmed black folks wouldn't be getting shot down in cold blood by militarized law enforcement officers.

White can't be right if a black president is OK. And if we can't take our conscious or unconscious frustrations out on him, we can take them out on folks who look like him.

For centuries, killing black folks in this country was hardly even illegal. Now that a black man is president, our primary preoccupation is condemning everything he does and buying more guns.

Sounds like we're whistling Dixie again.

Procreating from Beyond the Dead
The Paper of South Texas • *February 28, 2007*

On October 4, 1992, an eighteen-year-old dental assistant named Marion Ploch was driving to work near the German city of Erlangen. She lost control of her car and crashed into a tree. Local doctors spent the next four days trying to save her, but her fractured skull was too damaged.

While attempting to revive Ploch, doctors discovered that she was fourteen-weeks pregnant. The fetus was not harmed in the wreck and, though Ploch was declared brain-dead on October 8th, the doctors and Ploch's parents decided to keep her body alive with machines to see if the baby could develop enough in its mother's body to survive outside the womb.

On November 16, 1992, Marion Ploch's brain-dead body miscarried.

Fast forward fifteen years.

Israeli soldier Keivan Cohen was killed by a Palestinian sniper in 2002. He was single and left no will. At his parents' request, a sperm sample was taken from his dead body and stored in a hospital. When Cohen's family attempted to utilize the sperm for in vitro fertilization, the hospital refused access.

Fast forward five more years.

Austinite Kathleen Smith and her husband, U.S. Army Lieutenant Brian D. Smith, have a beautiful fifteen-month-old boy named Benton. He's the spitting image of his father who, sadly enough, has never met the boy. Brian died in Habbaniya, Iraq on July 2, 2004, after being shot by a sniper. When Benton was born, Brian had been dead for two years.

Kathleen and Brian had been trying in vitro fertilization before

Brian left for Iraq. It was agreed that Kathleen should continue the procedure while Brian was away. Kathleen was about to start a new in vitro fertilization attempt when she learned of her husband's death.

Brian Smith's parents were initially against Kathleen's continuance of the in vitro fertilization process because they were worried about her raising the child on her own and they were disturbed by the fact that Brian had no say in the matter. Kathleen's determination eventually won them over.

Keivan Cohen's parents won their lawsuit and, though the sperm taken from their dead son's body has been sitting in a cryo-preservation laboratory for almost five years, they plan to use a complete stranger as an incubator to "rebirth" some facsimile of Keivan.

Texan widow Kathleen Smith and the parents of Marion Ploch and Keivan Cohen all have two things in common. They all lost loved ones and they all simply tried to save some part of those loved ones or get some part of them back. But in as many ways as it's understandable, it's also disturbing.

What's Mrs. Smith going to tell Benton when he gets older? It throws the normal "boy meets girl, boy marries girl, boy and girl have baby" plotline out the window. In Keivan's case, boy never even meets girl. In Kathleen's case, boy does meet girl and marry her, but he dies way before girl has baby. Baby is the result of "postmortem" conception. If Ploch baby had survived, Ploch's plot would have read "girl meets boy, girl gets pregnant, girl dies--dead girl has baby."

Am I the only one who's creeped out by this?

Contemplating one's conception is always uncomfortable, even when it's natural. But when you introduce refrigeration processes, test tubes, inseminating syringes, court battles and unnatural procreation, don't you approach morbidity? And don't you lift the lid of Pandora's box just a little?

Don't get me wrong. I've always had contempt for the folks that stand around at funerals and refer to people's demises as "God's will." I think it's an immeasurable crock and, obviously, folks like the Plochs and the Cohens and Mrs. Smith agree.

But when does pro-activeness become ill-conceived Prometheanism?

The aims of Mrs. Smith. Mr. and Mrs. Ploch and Mr. and Mrs. Cohen were not ignoble, but neither were those of Dr. Victor Frankenstein. I am not suggesting in vitro fertilization or postmortem conception are monstrous, but somewhere Doc Frankenstein has to be smiling. And the lives resultant of such unconventional propagation may experience a painful "otherness" that most of us would never wish on the ones we loved.

The Cohens' lawyer, Irit Rosenblum, has called postmortem conception a "human revolution." Isn't it more than that? Doesn't it portend immortality and tease the fruition of Nietzsche's notion of the eternal return? Won't it permit do-overs, re-runs, after-the facts and *Boys from Brazil*-type stuff?

Is this what we really want?

What if the Bush or Clinton camps take note of this? Will it lead to a Bush or Clinton in the White House for eternity?

Natural Wisdom
Texas Co-Op Power • May 2015

Years ago, when I stood straighter and stepped more lightly, I was bent on staving off the responsibilities of adulthood. I did it by rambling cross-country, camping and hiking, sleeping on the ground and sometimes wandering for days and even weeks on end. A family and monthly bills finally caught up with me, but I still managed to sneak away regularly.

Inexorably, the years slowly encroached.

Now the ground feels harder, and a week away from my favorite pillow or chair is less appealing. I still have some "go" left in me, but not the same stride. It's frustrating, and I blame my dad.

In the late 1970s, I grew up surrounded by inklings of the future. Technology began to displace outdoor activities. Pay-per-view TV became popular, and Atari was all the rage. Microwave ovens appeared, and cassette tape players allowed us to record music off the radio. We still had bikes to ride and had to actually stand up to physically change the channels on the TV or the cartridge on the video game console, but the seeds of what was to come had already sprouted. We would slowly and incrementally become less active and spend less time outside after that. It seemed inevitable.

I don't think it bothered my father much because he had worked hard to expose us to outdoor experiences that left lasting impressions. But it must have registered on some level because it led to the greatest adventure of my young life.

My dad had taken me on canoe trips before, the first of which was down the Guadalupe River when I was seven or eight. But in 1979, just before I turned twelve, he took me on a ten-day river trek through the lower canyons of the Rio Grande, easily one of the most remote places in Texas.

No television, video games, microwaves, air conditioning, electricity, radio, telephone or tent—much less soft drinks or showers. We put in at the Boquillas Canyon Ranger Station of Big Bend National Park and plied for Langtry, roughly 160 miles east. We bathed in the river and drank from canteens. We cooked food over open fires and studied desert sky constellations for evening entertainment. If a rain interrupted our open-air slumbers, we rolled off our cots and slid underneath them and went back to sleep. If it got too hot on the river during the day, we took turns sliding into the water and drifting along with the canoe or banked our canoes and lounged under the shade of the cots.

My hands, previously most comfortable with a football, baseball glove or, more recently, an Atari controller, now brandished a wooden paddle, and I learned to navigate like a seasoned river rat.

In the quiet, crevassed solitude of the lower canyons, we could hear a serious rapid or waterfall at least a quarter of a mile away. We banked our canoe and hiked down to judge whether it was passable or if we needed to portage around it. I can't say our judgment was always correct or that we didn't luck through some tricky turns or get tumped over by a harrowing rock combination or two; but I can say I've experienced very little that compares to the exhilaration I felt during and after successfully traversing a rough whitewater stretch of the Rio Grande a little farther out than the middle of nowhere during that remarkable journey.

Today, I can hardly cross a bridge over a decent flowing river without thinking back to my time on the Rio. Technology and convenience are practically an inescapable part of our lives now, and that's fine. But it doesn't mean we shouldn't know our way around an oar or campfire or cot. It's easy to forget that the excitement and adventures we witness on a television, computer or cellphone screen are not actually happening to us, and that we're living them vicariously or virtually via the offspring of Atari and pay-per-view, instead of firsthand. I don't know whether my father knew or sensed what was coming or simply wanted to instill in me a sense of adventure, but our Rio jaunt put me way ahead of the curve. And I've tried to do the same with my children.

Texas has thousands of real-life experiences available at hundreds of state and national parks, rivers, lakes, waves, rocks, caves, canyons, deserts, mountains, forests, swamps and hike-and-bike trails. I've exposed my kids to as many as I could.

An adventure is always calling, and it's never too late, even if you've lost a step.

Slacking on the Taxpayers' Dime

Fort Worth Star-Telegram • March 22, 2009

It's a shame to see grownup, blue-collar folks taking naps, reading the newspaper or just sitting around all day, doing nothing at the American taxpayers' expense.

Stereotypically speaking, you might assume I'm referring to the unemployed multitudes who currently find themselves on some type of welfare. But you'd be only half right. The folks I'm referring to are on a type of welfare, but they aren't unemployed. They work for Lockheed Martin.

If you walk into Lockheed Martin's Fort Worth plant at any time on any given workday, you'll find an inordinate number of employees doing anything except work. You'll see people asleep in fuselages; taking repeated, extended coffee breaks; discussing the sports page; playing dominoes; and watching the clock. Anything to pass the time and make the day.

It's the ultimate gravy train, and you and I foot the bill.

Things have been that way out there for years, even back when the place was called General Dynamics. For the last few decades, only an embarrassing cross-section of the folks who work out there actually perform an honest day's labor and, in Lockheed Martin's case, this probably speaks to why its infamous Marine One helicopter and F-35 joint strike fighter are behind schedule and over budget.

But who's going to make waves?

When you've got a well-paying role in this kind of public fleecing, you don't get in a hurry.

You dutifully do less than your part regardless of delays or cost overruns, because the historical inefficiency and wastefulness of companies like General Dynamics, Lockheed Martin, Halliburton, Bell Helicopter, etc., pays the bills and then some.

You don't rock the boat when you're comfortable in it. And if you can get used to not doing much except collecting a paycheck, and you can it stick out for twenty to thirty years, you'll draw a fat pension with nice benefits on the taxpayers' nickel.

You have families out there for two and three generations, trotting after the easy money, voting for anyone who will keep one of Cowtown's most sacred cows producing.

When workers first show up, it's usually just a vocational detour. They're working at the plant until they can do something else.

But then they get comfortable. And patient. And then the easy money and long-term prospects for getting paid a lot to do very little takes the edge off their conscience.

The rest—excepting a union strike here and there—is simply a coast to the finish.

If you live in Fort Worth, none of this comes as a real shocker. I'm not revealing anything that most of us don't know. I just think we need to reconsider the state of affairs at our Lockheed Martin plant in the current context.

There are plenty of Lockheed Martin folks who work hard; but there are just as many who hardly work. And when we're in the process of reforming the domestic auto industry and criticizing it because it suffers from ineffective leadership, shoddy product development and too many built-in, wasteful labor costs, shouldn't we look real hard at the same profligate processes that take place in our back yard?

I hear lots of folks railing against bailouts and welfare programs these days, but what are the long-tolerated, wildly over-inflated price tags for weapons manufacturing—that pay many of our friends, family and neighbors to goof off all day—if not military-industrial welfare?

Lockheed Martin contends with unions just like American automakers, but if Lockheed's books start drifting into the red, the Pentagon just procures a budget increase. And if business is slow, the United States too coincidentally finds itself in another conflict or intervention or full-blown war. It often seems our military-industrial complex is just too big to fail.

Last year, as a nation, we spent more than a third of our overall budget on the Department of Defense and the war on terror.

We spent less than two percent on education and less than one percent on developing new energy strategies.

If companies like Lockheed Martin trimmed the fat off their operation, they'd save the taxpayers billions and free up funds for our paltry education and energy budgets.

This would obviously require streamlining the gravy train for many folks in Fort Worth, but surely they're tired of being on the government dole.

Made in Texas: Fake Boobs Turn Fifty

Dissident Voice • *March 10, 2011*

If I tell you I want to talk about fake boobs that came from the state of Texas, you're probably going to assume I'm referring to George W. Bush or Rick Perry. They're arguably the biggest pair of fake boobs we've seen around here in a long time, but they're not the fake boobs I'm talking about. I'm talking about the "trophy" wife variety. I'm talking about a major "cougar" accessory. I'm talking about the 50th anniversary of the Lone Star invention that changed American topography for good (or bad, depending on how you look at it).

The first breast augmentation processes popped up (pardon the pun) in the late 19th century. In 1889, Austrian physician Robert Gersuny tried paraffin injections. In 1895, German physician Vincenz Czerny placed tissue from a benign growth on a patient's back in a breast where he had removed a tumor to "avoid asymmetry."

In the first half of the 20th century, the race for the perfect fake boobs heated up. Well-apportioned actresses like Lana Turner and Ava Gardner were lighting up the big screen and gracing the covers of all the big-name magazines. Women and their husbands wanted topographical equality and doctors were eager to lend their talents and pad their bank accounts. By the late 40s, physicians were augmenting breasts with glass balls, ground rubber, ivory, ox cartilage, Terylene wool, gutta-percha, Dicora, polyethylene chips, polyvinyl alcohol-formaldehyde polymer sponge, polymer sponge in a polyethylene sac, polyether foam sponge, polyethylene strips wound into a ball, teflon-silicone, polyester rubber, etc.

In 1950, New York doctor Jacques Maliniac tried a "flap-based" augmentation and rotated a woman's chest wall tissue into her breast to increase volume. In the 1950s and early 1960s, approximately 50,000 women received silicone injections, but they led to dangerous granulomas and painful breast hardening.

In 1961, the first silicone breast implants were developed by Dr. Thomas Cronin and Dr. Frank Gerow, two plastic surgeons from Houston. They were made of a tear drop shaped rubber sac and filled with a thick, viscous silicone gel. They caught on in Hollywood first, because the price tag for the prosthetics was cost prohibitive. But, eventually, prices came down and they migrated back home.

Today, in most affluent areas in Texas, you can hardly stand in line at the supermarket or go watch your kids' basketball games without being confronted by trophy topography, and it's a little bit sad.

What happened to dancing with the ones that brung ya? Are the real things just not good enough for us anymore? And wasn't there a revolution in the 1970s that involved women railing against sexual objectification?

Is there any greater embrace of sexual objectification than fake boobs?

In the end I guess my own gender is most to blame. Gratuitous breast images sell us material goods and anchor the marketing campaigns for some of our favorite entertainment mediums. Even as adults, middle-aged dads and graying solitary or married men, we still lead with or can be led by our loins. And the bearings of our existential compasses are too often affected by women's breasts, real or fake.

Men are obviously pathetic for placing a premium on such things, and women are silly for caring so much about male premiums. Perhaps it's simply our nature but, if so, it's probably time for a little transcendence. Topographical transcendence.

It's often said that everything is bigger in Texas and, fifty years ago, two Houston doctors developed prosthetics to make sure such was the case. But their invention was a mockery of the Lone

Star quality of authenticity. And I'll take authenticity over artificiality any day.

When you get right down to it, fake boobs are about as attractive as toupees. And I don't know how folks are turned on by the former any more than the latter.

Just One Word: Water—
It's a Winning Investment

Fort Worth Star-Telegram, December 5, 2012

Can I get some advice from business-minded, investor types?

Two investment opportunities are available. The first involves investing short-term in a tried and true but finite resource. The investment will pay off more quickly, but it draws from a limited source.

The second investment involves investing long-term in an infinite resource, but it won't pay dividends immediately. When it begins to pay the dividends will be exponentially greater than those of the first opportunity and they'll last for centuries.

Which is the wiser investment?

This isn't a trick. I'm not peddling wind or solar energy.

The first investment opportunity is fossil fuels, but the second isn't a competing power source. It's water.

Right now debating the Keystone Pipeline from Canada to Texas is still the rage. It involves transporting crude oil from the Athabasca Oil Sands in Canada down to the Gulf Coast through Texas, to be refined and shipped off to foreign markets. Supporters of the project say it'll pay off like a slot machine and put thousands to work, but once the pipeline is done it will hardly employee hundreds. And we'll have invested in a diminishing resource that's bad for the environment and a Lone Star dead-end.

But water, we never have enough of that. Ninety-four percent of the state is abnormally dry and 54% is experiencing a severe drought. Last summer, the E.V. Spence Reservoir in West Texas south of Midland—normally a 14,600-acre lake up to 108 feet deep in places—was transformed into a muddy puddle no longer capable of meeting the needs of the 230,000 folks that rely on it. The surrounding landscape and local citizenry got mighty parched and state officials did little more than pray for rain.

Meanwhile, cities like Dallas were lobbying for a new dam on the Neches River in East Texas to supplement their H_2O demand. And in Fort Worth, the natural gas industry was using billions of gallons of water for fracking and possibly fouling billions more through the destabilization of injection wells caused by fracking-induced seismic activity. Water rationing programs were enacted and North Texans suffered through a dry one.

A new year won't a difference make. Dams and rationing aren't enough. They're simply quick fixes that will come back to haunt us. We need a pipeline or three in Texas, but not for crude oil. We need pipelines for water and we need to get that water from the Gulf of Mexico.

Texas' first permanent seawater desalinization plant is scheduled to open on the shores of South Padre Island in 2014. El Paso has been using desalinization processes to clean-up the brackish groundwater that comprises most of its water supply. And San Antonio has goals for a seawater desalinization plant and 140 miles of pipeline, but construction wouldn't start for decades.

Desalinization is not cheap. But neither is drought.

It's time to use our multi-billion dollar rainy-day fund to ensure "rain" and our state's reign as a prosperous, resourceful state. We need to invest in more desalinization plants along the Gulf and pipelines to bring water inland. Cities like Fort Worth and Dallas should join San Antonio, but speed up the process. In the long run, this type of investment will be profoundly more useful, profitable and job-stimulating than the Keystone imbroglio.

Desperately Seeking Intervention
Dissident Voice • November 3, 2011

How do you know if the community you live in is healthy? What are the symptoms of societal sickness?

Is civil strife a good indicator?

What about wide-scale despair or a prevalent lack of hope for the future?

In 2003, I spent some time in Cambodia. I crossed the border at Poi Pet and traveled up the main, red dirt highway to Siem Reap to visit Angkor Wat. It was one of the most uncomfortable journeys of my life.

I sat in the back seat of a cramped sedan and stared out the side windows. Every few hundred meters or so, on either side of the car, I saw warning signs indicating land mines. The hazard was communicated by a skull and crossbones symbol, and we passed hundreds if not thousands.

Cambodia is still dotted with six million land mines, remnants of the Vietnam War and the perilous reign of Pol Pot and the Khmer Rouge. The red dirt highway was relatively safe, and the communities that lie along it could be navigated by established paths, cleared by trial and error. But if you left the established paths, you took your life (and limbs) in your own hands. One in every 200 Cambodians is an amputee.

The ratio is staggering. And when you roam through local markets or bazaars, it is not uncommon to see begging double and triple amputees, dragging themselves along by their remaining limbs on the grimy pavement between market stalls.

Cambodia is a tragic, unsettling place. And the misfortune there is compounded by abject poverty, desperation and exploitation. It is not a healthy place to live; but neither is my country, though for far different reasons.

According to a recent report published by the Center for Disease Control and Prevention, one out of every 300 U.S. adults attempted suicide in the past year. That's 2700 a day, 100 per hour and almost two per minute. There were almost as many attempted suicides as abortions last year.

The two biggest reasons people attempt suicide are depression and psychosis. There are, of course, folks who harbor a sober, philosophical desire to die, whether to control their own destiny or alleviate suffering, but most are simply depressed or psychotic.

There's obviously plenty to be depressed or sick about in this country. We're not healthy. We're knowingly and willfully self-destructive in terms of our diets, our sedentary lifestyles and our environment. We're obsessively fixated on youthfulness and resort to injections and implants and try crèmes and pills to stay looking young—anything to avoid the appearance of wisdom.

We toil away at non-vital vocations that turn us into listless automatons. We're surrounded by technologies that allow us to communicate with everyone, but we rarely have anything reasonable or meaningful to say. Our nation and our species are going down the proverbial tubes and we have very little idea of what can be done about it.

We're obviously depressed. But when one in every 300 members of a nation's citizenry tries to kill themselves in a given year, it's time to consider whether individual depression isn't simply a symptom of collective psychosis.

One of the chief symptoms of psychosis is delusion. Victims harbor false beliefs that are persistent and organized and resistant to correction or logic.

Doesn't that describe us perfectly?

We believe what we want to believe regardless of the facts. We deny evolutionary theory even though our understanding of our own biology is based on it. We deny climate change even though its effects are already changing our existence. We believe that America is a good place to live even though success in our society is based more on ruthlessness than responsibility, and real honesty, in general, is considered naïve. And we insist the United States is still a great nation even though it hasn't been a positive force in the world for years.

Something is wrong with us.

We are depressed as a nation and psychotic as a people.

As the middle class—the chief bastion of normalcy and, arguably, decency, in our society—is slowly being amputated, our thought processes are confused. As our national glory fades, we talk now, mostly to ourselves. Our behavior is becoming strange and possibly dangerous, but we only absorb and process information that confirms our psychosis.

There needs to be intervention, but we protect our delusions with patriotic fervor. And we guard our dementia as if it were religion.

$th of July

Dissident Voice • *July 12, 2012*

Four years ago this month, a University of Minnesota student named Max P. Sanders was charged with bribery for putting his presidential vote up for sale on eBay.

The preceding May he had set a minimum bid of $10.00 for his presidential pick and offered to furnish photographic evidence of his eBay-bought choice in the voting booth. "Good luck!" he said in the listing. "Your country depends on You!"

The auction was something of a lark, of course, and Sanders received no offers. But the prank caught the attention of the Minnesota secretary of state's office and Hennepin County prosecutors were alerted. On July 3, 2008, Sanders was charged with one felony count of bribery under an 1893 state law that makes it a crime to offer to buy or sell a vote.

John Aiken, a spokesman for the Minnesota secretary of state's office said "There are people that have died for this country for our right to vote, and, to take something that lightly, to say, 'I can be bought'—it's a real shame."

The Hennepin county attorney on the case, Mike Freeman, concurred "A lot of us served in the military trying to protect the right to vote," he said. "This is serious stuff."

Well, yes. And no.

Mostly no. I'm sure many of you had as hard a time keeping a straight face reading this as I did writing it.

Bribery? Sold suffrage?

Has anybody been paying attention to Capitol Hill lately?

Corporate lobbyists spend hundreds of millions of dollars a year bribing our congressional representatives to cast votes that support heinous corporate indulgences and promote preposterous levels of corporate immunity. Billionaires spend hundreds of millions of dollars a year propping up puppet politicians to lick their boots in exchange for bottomless campaign coffers and cushy seats on corporate boards in their political afterlives. And our Supreme Court—via its Citizen's United decision—now enjoys its lowest approval rating ever for not just enabling the wholesale financial confiscation of our political system but actually sanctifying it.

Does the inescapable reality of our representative democracy being bought and sold every day really have to be pointed out? Don't most of us simply accept it now and expect it?

To be fair, the charges that came down against Sanders the day before the 4th of July in 2008 obviously smacked of an attempt at political point-scoring. But I can't help but go back to Aiken and Freeman's ridiculous indignation.

Does anyone really believe that the brave men and women Aiken and Freeman referred to fought for or sacrificed their lives for a nation where multinational corporate personhood holds more sway in the election booths than real, live, flesh and blood American citizens?

Does anybody honestly believe our soldiers knowingly and voluntarily risk their lives so our elections can be bought and sold by shadowy Capitalist entities?

The U. S. Supreme Court's Citizen's United rendering basically declared money a form of free speech and enabled corporations and billionaires to anonymously (and therefore freely) purchase political offices and pay for their say in our governance.

To some extent things may have always been thus, but now they're thusly so one hundred or one thousand fold.

We *can* be bought.

Our lives can be dictated by any frat-boy heir with a trust fund or three to spare.

So when you take a seat in a local ballpark or fold out a lawn chair near a public space to watch the community Fourth of July fireworks show, please ruminate a bit before the pyrotechnics start.

Yesterday, our flag wasn't emblazoned with a C-note. Yesterday, our real allegiance wasn't pledged to a stack of grubby cash.

Today we are one nation, under dollar signs, with liberty and justice for those who can afford it.

Our country no longer belongs to us, and it certainly no longer depends on us to be anything other than gullible, over-consuming, semi-sentient dupes.

Do we still live in a place where the right to vote is really worth fighting or dying for?

Soylent Green Will Be Stupid, Careless Morons
Dissident Voice, September 24, 2007

I grew up in the Seventies. It was a real primer for Armageddon.

Hollywood served up apocalyptic visions as often as networks today serve up reality shows. In 1971, *Omega Man* suggested that in the not too distant future, a plague would wipe out most of humankind and the survivors would battle Amish-leaning mutants for control of what's left. In 1972, *Silent Running* proposed that in the coming millenium Earth would no longer be suitable for plant-life and the remaining trees and plants would live in greenhouses on spaceships. In 1973, *Soylent Green* prophesied that by 2022, global food stores would be so depleted that the state would sanction suicide and we'd be eating our dead. In 1975, *Rollerball* suggested that by 2018, after the "Corporate Wars," the planet would be controlled by international business conglomerates that sponsor roller derby death matches instead of military bloodshed. In 1976, *Logan's Run* suggested that by the year 2274 we'd live beautifully and hedonistically in atmospheric bubbles until the ripe old age of thirty—at which time we'd be expected to submit to state-mandated termination.

And these grim scenarios all followed on the heels of *Planet of the Apes* (1968), which featured astronauts leaving earth in 1972 and returning in 3978 to find their fellow humans enslaved on a world ruled by apes, and *Beneath the Planet of the Apes* (1970), which introduced a telepathic human cult of fall-out survivors who worshipped a nuclear bomb.

If we didn't see these movies at the theatres, we saw the network premieres. If we didn't see the network premieres, we saw the reruns. And, as we only had five or six channels to choose from, we were all inculcated by the same doomsday projections.

Now, seven years into the new millennium, I find myself gauging the prescience of these sci-fi classics. I admit that they were often ludicrous and seriously flawed, but some of them may not have been as far-fetched as they seemed at the time.

Amish-leaning mutants probably won't be taking over any time soon, but we are a species ripe for a viral or bacterial cataclysm. Our immune systems are continuously being weakened by innumerable chemical toxins and growing economic, social and political stressors and, to compensate, we are over-vaccinating ourselves and popping antibiotics like *Flintstone* vitamins. Eventually we'll face a super-virus or super-bacteria that no amount of inflated health coverage will address, and our prescription-happy physicians will have no one left to over-medicate and our profit-mongering pharmaceutical companies will have no one left to price-gouge.

We're not sending Daffodils into space yet, but in recent years several bio-spheric chambers have been tested, NASA researchers have toyed with the idea of terra-forming Mars and, according to the 2007 Red List of Threatened Species (released on September 12th by the World Conservation Union), seventy percent of all known plant-life on Earth is threatened with extinction.

We aren't eating "Soylent Green" yet, but every year the number of communities in the world that permit doctor-assisted suicide grows, there's less and less room for cemeteries and millions of folks are going hungry or dying of starvation. Global food stores are being threatened by chaotic weather patterns, prolonged droughts, barren soils and a terrifying, new potential doomsday harbinger, bee colony-collapse disorder. We still have fifteen years to maneuver ourselves into *Soylent Green's* 2022 plotline and we may be right on track. In many places, folks are already drinking processed sewer water. How long before someone hits on the idea for recycling human flesh? *Bon Appétit!*

Roller derby death matches haven't caught on yet and may not by 2018, but nations like ours are governed by a corporate-controlled, military-industrial complex and giant corporate entities are involved in starting, prolonging and wildly profiting off "corporate" wars. With Capitalism spreading like a plague, there aren't enough resources to go around, so these wars will soon become commonplace. The planet probably won't be divvied up by 2018, but a fight over the Arctic Circle is brewing and soon no undeveloped or Third World real estate will be safe.

We're not living in self-contained, atmospheric bubbles, but if the hole in the Earth's ozone layer continues to grow we'll eventually need 150 SPF sunblock to mow the lawn. We're already turning more and more to cosmetic surgery (because no one wants to look like they're over thirty), we live as hedonistically as our credit cards allow and, once we pass our thirtieth birthday, we rapidly become the kind of dispensable adults we ourselves despised as children. We buy things we don't need, waste things we don't have enough of and elect scoundrels and idiots to represent, police, and govern us (With an electorate like us, who needs dictators?). Built-in termination dates would solve most of our health problems, allow us to scrap Social Security and put limits on the damage that lifelong ignorance, existential stagnation and the "good old days" syndrome does to our political system (SEE the 2000 presidential election; also, SEE the 2004 presidential election).

What does tomorrow hold? It's hard to say.

But we were warned.

The Real Scamps Behind the
Skull and Crossbones in the Indian Ocean
Dissident Voice • *December 7, 2009*

A couple of weeks back, I saw that the United States was now sending remote-controlled MQ-9 Reaper planes to patrol the Indian Ocean in search of Somali pirates. Apparently the destitute Somalis have "Kick Me" signs attached to their backs and the United States is going down there to tee them up.

We weren't sending Reapers to patrol the area when the Italians, Germans or Swiss were dumping toxic waste off the coast of Somalia. We had no intentions of getting involved when the dumping we ignored was stirred up by the tsunami of 2004 and toxic waste tanks began washing up on Somali beaches and fouling the coastal ecosystem. And we weren't bothered when Somalis in the area began suffering from radiation sickness, cancer outbreaks and harrowing birth defects. It wasn't our problem, and it wasn't any of our business.

We also didn't care that even before the dumping, several of our Asian and European cohorts were illegally exhausting Somali fisheries, leaving hundreds of thousands of Somali fisherman without livelihoods. Somalia had no functional government much less Coast Guard, so the entire state was an easy mark. When Somalis were being put upon, they were just a nameless, faceless multitude whose fate was none of our concern. But when bands of nameless, faceless Somali fisherman began resorting to piracy because they no longer had any viable means of supporting their families, then we started paying attention. And when First World cargo ships were seized and British jet-setters got kidnapped from their yachts, well, that was too much. America had to step up.

None of this stuff is really news because nothing about it is really new. A people or a country is denied some of the basic rights and considerations that you and I (and most other First World citizens) enjoy and take for granted. They resent this treatment and rebel or attempt to take matters into their own hands. We put them down (or help someone else put them down) as if they are the transgressors, as if they are the ones who perpetrated the original offense. It's been the bedrock of our foreign policy for the last forty years. We have no problem portraying the victims as the assailants and making it our patriotic duty to coerce them, punish them or bomb them back to the Middle Ages if they don't start marching to the tune of our cash registers.

Thusly, the coast of Somalia has been transformed into a First World dumping station. A contingent of our allies fished it clean and then flushed their industrial waste there. The natives had little or no recourse, so our allies simply did as they pleased.

Luckily, world opinion deems the Somalis "pirates" instead of peasants, and this allows us to condemn the proactive victims in good conscience and hunt them down like criminals.

It doesn't matter that this is an example of some of the proverbial excrement that floats around in First World punchbowls. There are not enough resources to go around, so someone's going to do without. And the folks who have access to the most resources will produce the most waste and they'll need somewhere to put this waste. Where better than the home of the folks who have access to the fewest resources?

Advocates of Capitalism and Social Darwinism say that it's just the Third World's lot in life. Too bad, so sad. And as we grow fat in our LazyBoys, listening to our flat screen TVs remind us how great we are, we sometimes almost care about those less fortunate than us. But then Tiger sinks a twenty-five-foot put or a couple on *Dancing with the Stars* receives a perfect score. And the Somalis have no right to piracy.

We don't mind them being treated like animals as long as they refrain from retaliatory wherewithal. That's where we draw the line.

In the old world, the skull and crossbones symbolized piracy. In the modern world, the skull and crossbones are the internationally recognized symbol for poison. How is utilizing the former worse than destroying a people's habitat or way of life with the latter? I don't condone piracy or violence, but I'm appalled that my country is taking the side of the malefactors in this matter. And if I was a Somali living along the Indian Ocean instead of a dupe atrophying in front of a flatscreen, I don't think I'd take losing my livelihood or watching my children suffer from radiation poisoning lightly. In fact, I'd probably join the bad guys. Especially the ones on my side.

Of Mice and Meaning

Aledo Community News • *August 24, 2012*

A week or so ago, I got out of town.

Away from work. Away from the general conundrum.

I even enjoyed a respite from electronica.

Camping just west of Junction, Texas, I had no TV, radio or service for my cell phone. Every evening deer wandered into and around my camp. We regarded each other demurely.

I took a midnight dip in the South Llano River on August 12th and watched the beginning of the Perseid Meteor Shower as the cool water soothed the day's sunburn. It was a mystical moment that reminded me of the galaxy's incredible rhythm and spectacle.

If I wasn't off the grid, I was at least on a remote corner of it, and it felt good. But the over-inhabited world has a way of catching up to you, even in faraway places.

Later that next morning, I'd grabbed a copy of the *Junction Eagle* to peruse the regional comings and goings. I liked to get as familiar with a locale as a short jaunt allowed me, and a local newspaper was always the best place to start. But something in the *Eagle* immediately caught my eye and put me right back in the middle of grids and conundrums.

It was an ad published in the lower left-hand corner of the front page by the "Parents for Academic Success." The gist of it was listed in the first full paragraph of copy. It said: "The summer reading program in the AP English classes at JISD has books whose contents are offensive to the Christian religion. After months of deliberation and complaints to the administration and school board concerning vulgar and immoral content, the books remain as required reading."

Then, skipping a way's down: "The contents of these books create an offensive educational environment, affecting some students' ability to participate in the educational program, and thereby, affecting the students' educational opportunities."

The splendid images of coy deer and Perseid flares exited my mind like fleeing criminals.

There's a big difference between knowing there are pockets of close-mindedness in this country and actually stumbling onto them unawares.

On the way back home a day or so later, I called the *Junction Eagle* and asked them the names of the "offensive" books. They identified them as *Beloved* by Toni Morrison, *Speak* by Laurie Halse Anderson and John Steinbeck's *Of Mice and Men*.

For the uninitiated, *Beloved* is a haunting story that deals with the psychological repercussions of slavery. It won the Pulitzer Prize for Fiction in 1988. *Speak* details a young woman's attempt to move on after being raped by a popular classmate the summer before her freshman year in high school. In 1999 it was a National Book Award finalist; in 2000 it was named a Best Book for Young Adults by the American Library Association. It also won the Society of Children's Book Writers and Illustrators' Golden Kite Award for Fiction and was named a Printz Honor Book.

Of Mice and Men, originally published seventy-five-years ago to broad and lasting critical acclaim, is a novella that follows the tragic story of two displaced migrant ranch workers during the Great Depression. Despite being one of the most banned books of the 20th and early 21st centuries—for wrongheaded charges of promoting euthanasia, racism and anti-Capitalist sentiments—*Of Mice and Men* has been on high school and college reading lists for decades. So what gives? Or, better put, what gives narrow-minded zealots the right to take books away from children?

As I understand it, the point of education is not simply to confirm what we already know or have had experience with. In fact, it's often quite the opposite. A good education teaches us new things and often requires us to experience things differently or consider different experiences. And this is probably especially true in AP English classes, where the reading material is advanced and more challenging.

My brief sojourn into Kimble County was not part of a school lesson, but it was educational and enlightening. And fulfilling.

If I had been discouraged from camping near Junction or standing in the South Llano River on August 12, I might have missed out on some wonderful experiences. If I hadn't left my air conditioned home or stepped outside of my secure conundrum on the grid, I wouldn't have experienced things differently.

And so with reading *Beloved*, *Speak* or *Of Mice and Men*. The narratives take us into contexts most of us are remarkably unfamiliar with. Morrison, Anderson and Steinbeck invite us to see how different folks in different times and different places may have experienced things, broadening our perspective and widening our scope—of participation and involvement.

To my knowledge, Aledo ISD—my alma mater and the future alma mater of my children—has never attempted to ban a book. It certainly never happened while I was enrolled there and I have heard no mentions of such.

This heartens me and should comprise no small source of local pride.

Padlocking books is not a good way to unlock a child's potential. There are as many adventures and experiences to be had in books as there are on rivers and roads and we should never attempt to deprive each other of either.

One of my children, a daughter, begins high school in a few days. I think she should read *Speak* posthaste. She's also mixed, Anglo- and African-American. So maybe *Beloved* after *Speak*. A little history never hurts. Steinbeck is a giant of American letters; she'll cross him soon enough.

In the meantime, she was with me to see the deer and the meteor shower. And she'd read half the books on the AHS freshman AP English summer reading list by the time she was eleven.

Legion of Doom-kopfs

Fort Worth Weekly • April 18, 2012

OK. Tell me if this sounds familiar.

There's this group of Anglo-Americans, mostly well-to-do and some wealthy. They're not big fans of minorities (especially African-Americans) or the poor. They detest homosexuals. They feel they know better than the rest of us what's best for the community, so they've anointed themselves as the right folks to restore order and clean things up.

Republican Party 2012?

No.

Well, yes. But conservatives of the new millennium are not the ones I had in mind. I was actually thinking back to Paschal High School in Fort Worth, Texas, circa 1985. I was remembering the Legion of Doom.

By all accounts, members of Paschal High's Legion of Doom were All-American guys from good, mostly privileged families, some even inhabiting the rarefied confines of the Tanglewood and Overton Park neighborhoods on the West Side.

The Legion of Doom didn't like the growing minority population at Paschal. They didn't like the increased levels of theft and drug use that they attributed to this increase. So, based on a misguided, self-indulgent sense of righteous indignation, these clean-cut, flag-waving Caucasian students decided to do something about it.

They threatened classmates with guns and shot out a local porch light with an M-1 carbine. They vandalized lockers and used a black-painted dummy for target practice. They built a homemade bazooka and a gasoline bomb. They denigrated poor kids and homosexuals, pipe-bombed a classmate's car, and left a gutted cat splayed across another's steering wheel.

The hateful antics of the Legion, and its members' subsequent indictments and trials, were well-reported in the 1980s. But what didn't get much coverage were the Legion's philosophical under-pinnings. Members of the Legion were conservative athletes and honor students. They were strait-laced sons of lawyers and exec-utives and even one Christian minister. As one member's mother put it, they were all "pro-Republican."

And the relevance of the Legion of Doom's political leanings should never be downplayed.

The Ronald Reagan presidency ushered in an alarming up-tick in all things conservative, and many Republicans—especially those who had hung their heads in shame since Watergate—were fat and sassy again. As pop act Huey Lewis and the News so aptly phrased things, it was once again "hip to be square."

But the Legion obviously took things too far. Their victims had had a hard enough time trying to act white or straight or up-per-middle class; demanding that they be square or else just add-ed insult to the many injuries the Legion inflicted.

All these years later, of course, it simply seems that the Legion of Doom was just ahead of its time.

In a society where abortion providers are gunned down in church, politicians are shot in public, and African-American teen-agers are killed for being black, the Legion of Doom today almost seems tame. They might even be a hit with hardcore Republicans and would undoubtedly be hailed by blowhards like Rush Lim-baugh as good, misunderstood Americans (like him).

We live in troubling times. It seems that for every sane person you run into, you meet two wackos. And not Charlie Manson or Jeffrey Dahmer wackos. I'm referring to Ward and June Cleaver wackos. I'm talking about Mayberry freaks. A large percentage of Middle America appears to have gone zombie and can only be sated by gorging on hatred and fear.

In the 1980s, a sociology professor from Texas Christian Uni-versity noted that Legion members' self-image as well-meaning vigilantes working to rid their community of destructive elements smacked of a rationalization "to soothe their conscience."

Smells like team spirit in the trenches of the 2012 Republican base.

A black man is president. Women's reproductive rights have strengthened their independence. Gays are allowed to fight for their country. The nation is becoming more open-minded and diverse.

In places like Arizona, Virginia, and Texas, the right is pushing back, encouraging voter disenfranchisement efforts, trans-vaginal intimidation, etc. Another legion is overstepping its bounds.

When will we fight back?

Create Dangerously: A Call to Artistic Arms

Dissident Voice • December 23, 2010

On January 19, 1919, Vaslav Nijinsky, the greatest dancer of the 20th century, performed a special wartime recital at the Suvretta House Hotel in St. Moritz, Switzerland. Leading up to the event, he refused to say what he intended to dance and wouldn't even give hints as to the accompaniment. He was, after all, a star of the highest magnitude. He influenced culture, fashion and society and his appearance would draw a crowd regardless of the presentation.

When the recital started, he performed some perfunctory turns and flashed his mastery in a few signature aerials. Then he grabbed a chair and abruptly sat down facing his audience.

Nijinsky glared at them. Time passed but the audience was silent. More time passed and still Nijinsky stared.

The audience sat motionless.

After several minutes, Njinsky rose. He took rolls of black and white velvet and made a giant cross the length of the room. Then he stood at the head of it with open arms and said: "Now I will dance you the war, with its suffering, with its destruction, with its death. The war which you did not prevent and so you are responsible for."

And then Nijinsky erupted across the room, his monumental gestures filling the space with horror and suffering. The audience was breathless, fascinated and petrified. Nijinsky's movements and expressions suffused the room with twisted, contorted bodies and savage explosions. He took his audience to the trenches, the front, and the body-strewn aftermath. He was ethereal and violent, a perfect embodiment of tragic, terrible humanity.

His audience was discomfited, but undeniably moved. His recital was intense, brilliant and compelling.

If you go to the neighborhood library or check *Wikipedia*, you may find Nijinsky as a historical figure or a physical genius. But you will hardly find the spirit of the phenomena the aforementioned dance represented. And it's entirely absent on the TV channels and radio stations and art galleries we frequent today. They are devoid of urgency and sadly lack the cogent, poetic ferocity that comprised Nijinsky's St. Moritz performance.

Contemporary pop culture is virtually bereft of real relevance and depth and the corporate architects who promote it go to extraordinary lengths to keep it that way. Taylor Swift is as challenging as a lukewarm bath. Lil Wayne is as evocative as a mustard burp. And Justin Bieber is as meaningful as soggy bread crust crumbs in mayonnaise.

Sure, there's a Sinead O'Connor tearing up the Pope's picture here and there or a Sharon Olds addressing "The Solution" we seem to have chosen for ourselves. And now and then we hear a Rage Against the Machine; but the Bob Dylans are desperately missed. There's no future in banal Beyonces, toothless Labeoufs or spineless *Twilight* and Harry Potter sequels.

There's no edge to our art anymore because it's filled with entertainers instead of artists and the few artful souls that do unintentionally get featured usually lack awareness or philosophy.

Kurt Vonnegut used to say that artists were like canaries in a coal mine. That they were super-sensitive and "keeled over" due to toxic conditions long before normal folks even sensed they were in danger. Vonnegut envisioned art as an indispensable herald, a critical means of alarm.

But despite the unparalleled toxicity of our times and our complicity in the systems that endanger us, artists aren't sounding the alarm. There are as many doom-impending calamities in the world now as there are countries, but most artists are hardly even sentient, much less super-sensitive.

French existentialist Albert Camus went further than Vonnegut. He plainly stated that "the time for irresponsible artists is over" and that in any troubled era, it was every legitimate artist's role to create dangerously.

Today we are involved in one war and one quasi-occupation, but no performer on any significant stage or medium is dancing the war for us or compellingly conveying the shabbiness or shame of the occupation. Our socio-economic system is exposing us to a catalog of environmental perils, but our creative communities spend more time cashing in on the system than condemning it. Our technological dependence is rendering an inestimable number of our natural, physiological capacities obsolete, but more artists are turning to the new, dehumanizing technologies than disputing their real, long-term merit.

Art for art's sake was fine when there was nothing at stake, but when everything is at stake artistic expression demands courage and accountability. So if you fancy yourself a literary or filmic or singing sort and your muse isn't telling you to dance our inhumanities or paint our self-destructiveness or pen our vainglorious insanities, please ignore it and find another pursuit among the uninitiated throngs. We already have enough artists who create safely.

An Immodest Proposal
Fort Worth Weekly • February 23, 2011

Tell me if this sounds familiar.

The U.S. trains another country's paramilitary forces to wage war against American enemies. Those forces do fight U.S. enemies but later change sides to become a different, perhaps greater menace, and the U.S. military finds itself battling combatants that they themselves have trained.

Take a guess at what country I'm talking about.

Afghanistan?

Good guess. Try again.

Iraq?

Not as good a guess as Afghanistan, but not bad.

The Afghans were our surrogate soldiers against Russia in the early 1980s. We armed them and trained them as best we could. We even instructed a young jihadist named Osama bin Laden.

We also supplied and trained some of Saddam Hussein's forces in their late-1980s campaigns against Iran. Then, when we went over there for the first Gulf War, we faced some of the same weaponry we'd provided them just a few years earlier. But that was a long time ago.

The success of the late Bush administration surge in Iraq had nothing to with anybody we trained. It was primarily achieved by paying enemy combatants to stay home and keep carnage on the down-low so things could settle down and we could look good in the press.

The most recent example of Uncle Sam spending our tax dollars on attack animals that turn on their handlers isn't happening in the Middle East or the Money-Pit on Terror. It's happening right here in North America, and Texas has a front-row seat. We're now battling another band of U.S. military-trained combatants on our border with Mexico.

The core members of the Zetas, a drug-muscle splinter group that used to do the dirty work for the Gulf Cartel, were trained in special ops, counter-narcotic ops, counter-insurgency, light to heavy weapons proficiency, and covert communications at Ft. Bragg, N.C., by the U.S. 7th Special Forces group in the 1990s. They worked for the Mexican armed forces for a while, but the good guys didn't pay enough, so they switched sides. Then they decided they could run things better than the Gulf Cartel, and now they're the scariest border presence in the Mexican drug war. Whole towns exist without law enforcement. The populations of entire cities are afraid to go out after dark.

The Zetas don't spare women and children; they don't even spare pregnant women.

Boy, we sure know how to pick 'em.

When is Uncle Sam going to stop using psychopaths as errand boys? *And shouldn't we finally admit that Uncle Sam is something of a psychopath himself?*

Hold those thoughts.

What if we simply met with our former trainees in the Zetas and offered to pay them to kick back with Tecates at the beach in Matamoras or Vera Cruz? It worked in Iraq.

Even better, what if we recalibrated their American-trained, psychopathic bloodlust to once again work in our favor?

Right now, the drug trade across the U.S.-Mexico border is considered to be worth $20 billion to $40 billion, and the Zetas don't have a big piece of it. Illegal immigrants are bringing unwanted attention to border drug routes, and our efforts to stop them have been about as effective as the Army Corps of Engineers' levees in New Orleans. The "gringos' little helper" trade has to cross our southern border, so why not simply enlist the Zetas to police both flows of traffic?

The Zetas want more of a foothold in the narcotics market, and we don't like their friends and neighbors sneaking over into this country to have babies and steal our jobs. If the Zetas controlled the border, they could get our drugs to us with less expense and headache, and we could start getting baked for a song. And with the Zetas as U.S. border guards, their fellow countrymen would be too terrified to cross them by crossing the border, especially if the Zetas started stitching the immigrants' skinned faces on soccer balls or placing the heads of women and children on pikes.

Heck, we could even make the Zetas a government-subsidized branch of Blackwater (a.k.a. Xe Services, LLC), and then their ruthlessness would be legitimized.

God bless American ingenuity.

A Forgotten Slaughter of African Americans in Texas

Dissident Voice, February 25, 2013

Last month marked the 90th anniversary of the Rosewood Massacre in Florida and calls a similar Texas slaughter to mind.

The 1923 Rosewood Massacre saw six blacks and two whites killed. The 1910 Slocum Massacre in East Texas reportedly saw eight to twenty-two blacks killed and no whites. The Rosewood Massacre is remembered as a national tragedy, even receiving Hollywood treatment; the Slocum Massacre has become a dirty Lone Star secret, remarkable more for the inattention it's received than its remembrance.

Unlike most Texas and Anderson County communities in the early 20th century, the unincorporated town of Slocum—like Rosewood—was largely African American, with several black citizens considerably propertied, and a few owning stores, businesses, etc. This alone, in parts of the south, might have been enough to foment violence. But in the Slocum area, which included the small communities of Priscilla and Denson Springs, there were other issues.

When a white man tried to collect a disputed debt from a well-regarded black citizen, a confrontation occurred and hard feelings lingered. When a regional road construction foreman put an African American in charge of gathering up help for some local road improvements, a prominent white citizen named Jim Spurger was infuriated and became a vociferous agitator.

Rumors began to spread, warning of threats against Anglo citizens and plans for race riots. White malcontents manipulated the local Anglo population and, on July 29th, white hysteria transmogrified into bloodshed.

Stoked and goaded by Spurger and others, hundreds of Anglo citizens from all over Anderson County converged on Slocum armed with pistols, shotguns and rifles. That morning, near Sadler Creek, they fired on three African Americans headed to feed their cattle, killing eighteen-year-old Cleveland Larkin and wounding fifteen-year-old Charlie Wilson. The third, eighteen-year-old Lusk Holly, escaped, only to be shot at again later in the day while he, his twenty-three-year-old brother Alex and their friend William Foreman, were fleeing to Palestine. Alex was killed and Lusk was wounded. Foreman fled and disappeared. Lusk pretended to be dead so a group of twenty white men would not finish him off.

White mobs marched through the area shooting black folks at will. A thirty-year-old African-American named John Hays was found dead in a roadway and twenty-eight-year-old Sam Baker was shot to death in front of his house. When three of the Baker's relatives (Dick Wilson, Jeff Wilson and a seventy-year-old man named Ben Dancer) attempted to sit up with his body the following night, they, too, were gunned down in cold blood. According to an August 1 report in the *Galveston Daily News*, bloodstains at the residence indicated they were shot on the front porch and then dragged inside.

In addition to the Anderson County murders, which occurred near the county line, Will Burley was killed in Houston County.

According to the August 1 edition of the *Newark Daily Advocate*, the mobs traveled from house to house, shooting African Americans who answered their calls and slaughtering more while they tended their fields.

Every early newspaper report (in the *New York Times*, *Galveston Daily News*, *Fort Worth Star-Telegram*, et al.) on the transpiring bloodshed in and around Slocum portrayed the African Americans as armed insurrectionists that the local Anglo community was simply defending itself against. These accounts were gross mischaracterizations. When district judges in Palestine closed saloons and ordered local gun and ammunition stores to stop selling their wares on July 30, it was not to quell a Black uprising; it was to defuse what the *Galveston Daily News* called an indescribable, one-sided "reign of terror" characterized by "a fierce manhunt in the woods" and resulting in "riddled bodies found on lonesome roads."

When reporters gathered on July 31, up to two dozen murders had been reported and more were suspected, but local authorities only had eight bodies. Once the carnage had begun, hundreds of African-American's had fled to the surrounding piney woods and local marshes. By the time the Texas Rangers and state militia arrived, there was no way to estimate the number of African American dead.

On August 1, a few Texas Rangers and other white men gathered up six of the African American bodies and buried them (wrapped in blankets and placed in a single large box) in a pit four miles south of Slocum. Farther north, Marsh Holly, father of Alex and Lusk, was found on a road just outside Palestine. He was terrified and begged the authorities in Palestine for help, requesting that he be locked up in jail for protection. He identified himself as the well-regarded black citizen involved in the promissory note dispute, but denied that the affair comprised a serious provocation.

After the first several murders, much of the African American community attempted to flee the area, but this didn't stop the white mobs. They shot down blacks they discovered in the countryside, even if they were clearing out. Two bodies found near the town of Priscilla still had travel bundles of food and clothing at their sides.

Anderson County Sheriff William H. Black said it would be "difficult to find out just how many were killed" because they were "scattered all over the woods." He also admitted that buzzards would find many of the victims first, if at all.

It's reasonable to suspect that after the initial bloodlust had subsided, some of the transgressors returned to the murder scenes to remove the evidence of their crimes. Certainly with the arrival of the press—and after early attempts at spinning the news reports to portray the African American victims as armed insurrectionists had failed—the guilty Anglo contingents engaged in damage control efforts. But Sheriff Black was inexorable and unflinching.

"Men were going about killing Negroes as fast as they could find them," Black told the *New York Times*. "And, so far as I was able to ascertain, without any real cause."

"These Negroes have done no wrong that I can discover," Black continued. "I don't know how many [whites] were in the mob, but there may have been 200 or 300. Some of them cut telephone wires. They hunted the Negroes down like sheep."

According to the local law enforcement leaders on hand at the time, eight casualties was a conservative number. Sheriff Black and others insisted there were at least a dozen more and some reports suggest there may have been dozens more. Elkhart native F. M. Power said there were thirty "missing negroes." Slocum-area resident Luther Hardeman claimed to have knowledge of eighteen African American casualties, and that's the original number reported by the *Galveston Daily News* and the *New York Times* (on July 31), but the body count seemed to shrink as the massacre's publicity grew. A reliable fatality count was impossible, especially with the perpetrators likely covering their tracks. And the deceased weren't the only folks becoming scarce; the remaining, surviving African Americans began to disappear as well.

It was one thing to return to your home or your daily routine after the odd murder or infrequent lynching of one of your friends, neighbors or relatives—black folks in the south were not unused to that. But a localized campaign of genocide, where the executioners surrounded you and cut phone lines to prevent you from getting help? That was not something Slocum-area African Americans could easily relegate to a list of bygones.

If the proverbial water under the bridge was auburn with African American blood, home was no longer a place to return to. And with a large contingent of the black community running for their lives, some victims went unidentified and some disappearances went unreported.

The arrival of the Texas Rangers and the state militia stabilized the situation or at least made it safe enough for many of the remaining African Americans to pack their belongings and leave without being fired on. The saloons in Anderson County were re-opened for business at noon on August 1.

When a *Galveston Daily News* correspondent visited Lusk Hol-ly and Charlie Wilson on July 31 (two days before their Grand Jury testimony), they were both suffering incredible levels of pain due to the gunshot wounds they had received. The correspondent re-ported that their injuries would be "relieved only by death unless medical attention is speedily afforded." Wilson had a fractured thigh, damage to one ankle and "glancing wounds through his chest." Holly had eight to ten pieces of buckshot in his lower left abdominal area and damage to one arm. Physicians had perfunc-torily treated their wounds when they were first discovered two days prior, but not since.

Wilson told the *Galveston Daily News* correspondent that he had recognized two of the assailants during the first shooting on July 29. Holly said that after he had been wounded in the sec-ond shooting later in the day, a different group of white men had come upon him while he pretended to be dead. He said he recog-nized the voice of a prominent, local farmer named Jeff Wise, who deemed his apparent and his brother's actual death "a shame" as he passed by.

In the weeks and months following what came to be known as the Slocum Massacre, the African American population made a mass exodus, leaving homes, properties, businesses and personal connections to the land and the community.

At the initial Grand Jury hearing, nearly every remaining Slo-cum resident was subpoenaed; some residents refused to testify and were arrested. The Grand Jury judge, B.H. Gardner, of Pal-estine, told the all-male, all-white jury that the massacre was "a disgrace, not only to the county, but to the state" and it was up to them to do their "full duty."

According to the August 2 edition of the *Palestine Daily Herald*, Judge Gardner attempted to clarify the charges and the issues at hand, explaining various statutes to the jury. He said that even if there had been threats or conspiracies "on the part of any number of Negroes to do violence to white persons, it would not justify anybody to take the law into their own hands."

"The law furnishes ample remedy," Gardner continued. "There is no justification for shooting men in the back, waylaying or killing them in their houses."

When the Grand Jury findings were reported on August 17, several hundred witnesses had been examined. Though eleven men were initially arrested and seven were finally indicted, only six were named—and they were only accused in the murders of five of the identified victims. Defendants Reagon McKenzie, T. W. Bailey and Morgan Henry were released without being charged. Jim Spurger was indicted in two cases, B. J. Jenkins in four cases and Curtis Spurger, Steve Jenkins, Isom Garner and Andrew Kirkwood in three cases. The seventh indicted man was not arrested or named; only Kirkwood was immediately granted bail. No one was ever indicted for the deaths of John Hays or Alex Holly.

After the Grand Jury indictments came down, Judge Gardner decided to move the trial for the indicted, identified perpetrators of the Slocum Massacre to Harris County, distrusting the potential jury of peers the defendants might receive in Anderson County. The indictments received no interest in Harris County.

On May 4, 1911, Judge Ned R. Morris of Palestine petitioned the Travis County Court of Criminal Appeals to grant bail for the remaining defendants and it was granted. Eventually, all those charged were released and none of the indictments were ever prosecuted.

In the meanwhile, the personal holdings of many Slocum area Anglo citizens fortuitously increased.

The abandoned African American properties were absorbed or repurposed as the now majority white population saw fit. The standard southern Anglo-centric world order was restored, and this order has endured, even to the present day.

According to recent demographic statistics, most of the communities around Slocum have an African American population that ranges between 20-25%. Grapeland's is 35%, Rusk's is 30% and Palestine's and Alto's is 25%. Slocum's African American population is just under 7%.

Today, Slocum is still an unincorporated community and that's probably wise. If there was an elected civic leader or assembly in Slocum, they might be asked to apologize for the massacre or explain why there are no placards acknowledging the event or the American citizens who were slaughtered there and covered up in unmarked graves in the woods and creek bottoms.

On April 24, 1929, a tornado rolled through Slocum, leveling the town, killing seven and injuring 20. Organizations from all over East Texas went to great lengths to raise money for the victims and help the town get back on its feet. Though the Slocum Massacre's casualties were greater and its African American community's coerced migration was arguably just as landscape-altering, the twister overshadowed the localized genocide of 1910, and the event is largely forgotten today.

In the Rosewood Massacre, six blacks and two whites were killed and a special, governor-appointed grand jury found no one to prosecute. In the Slocum Massacre, at least eight blacks were killed and no whites were even injured and, though seven men were indicted by a grand jury, none were ever prosecuted. In both cases, thriving African American populations vacated their own communities to survive a racially-motivated bloodbath.

In the *Rosewood Victims v. the State of Florida* decision in 1994, Florida became the first U.S. State to compensate the victims and the descendants of victims of racial violence and, ten years later, the site of Rosewood was designated a Florida Heritage Landmark.

In Texas, the Slocum Massacre—which was at least as heinous as the Rosewood Massacre—hasn't even received a historical marker. And there have been no investigations to determine the toll of the carnage, the extent of the personal losses or the exact number of victims.

On March 30, 2011, after a February 27 story on the Slocum Massacre in the *Fort Worth Star-Telegram* (by Tim Madigan), the 82nd Texas Legislature adopted House of Representatives Resolution 865 (filed by Reps. Marc Veasey and Lon Burnam), acknowledging the Slocum Massacre of 1910. It admitted that a mob comprised of hundreds of armed white men in the Slocum area went on a "bloody rampage" that resulted in eight and perhaps many more African-American deaths, forcing the black community there to abandon their homes and properties and flee. The resolution concluded with flowery language stating that "only by shining a light on previous injustices can we learn from them and move forward," but the little-publicized gesture hardly accomplishes that.

In testimony presented at the bail hearing on May 10, 1911, defense witness Alvin Oliver criticized the "insolent manner and conduct" of the blacks in that part of Anderson County after the lynching of an African American in neighboring Cherokee County a couple of years before and brazenly noted that things were different after the massacre.

"The Negroes down there are not disbehaving now," Oliver observed.

And he was right.

There were hardly any left.

NOTE: In 2015, author E. R. Bills and Constance Hollie-Jawaid, a descendant of Slocum Massacre victims, got a historical marker acknowledging the Slocum Massacre approved by the Texas Historical Commission. It was erected in the Slocum area in late December 2015 and dedicated on January 16, 2016.

Isle of Blight

Fort Worth Weekly • May 21, 2008

Hundreds of miles out in the Pacific Ocean between Hawaii and San Francisco, a new mass has appeared that scientists say is about twice the size of Texas. Visions of Lemuria, the Pacific version of Atlantis come to mind—maybe another island neighbor that we could invade and claim!

But before you get too excited about lost continents or imperialistic opportunism, you should know that the new mass is 80 percent plastic—mostly mainland trash—and that it's commonly referred to as the Great Pacific Garbage Patch. It has been roiling and growing out there for years, getting bigger and wider—*but, hey, out of sight out of mind, right?*

Especially for us. We don't even live on the West Coast; we live in Fort Worth, where the West begins.

Unfortunately, the West begins kind of like it ends. As you drive out west on Camp Bowie Boulevard, you see your first large, rolling prairie hill on the skyline to your right, with what looks like a road running down the side. Actually, it's a plastic-lined runoff ditch, and the "prairie hill" is a man-made mound, built to conceal a waste disposal site. The sign in front of the mound says "Westside Transfer Station," better known as a landfill.

Behind the pseudo-prairie hill are tons and tons of the residue of our existence. We put it in bags, drop the bags in trash cans, put the cans out next to the curb and—*presto!* When we get home from work, the cans are empty and ready to refill.

Like so many processes and phenomena that play a part in our lives, we don't concern ourselves with end results. We simply focus on convenient means. We have mouths to feed, lives to lead, and places to be, so we embrace any process or product that increases our existential leisure, regardless of whether it's environmentally destructive, wasteful, or toxic.

A few years back, my parents asked me to take a load of brush they had cut down on their property out to the Westside dump. I paid at the gate and drove up the hill. Once atop it, a panorama of piled garbage was revealed, populated by bulldozers pushing the refuse into a pit.

If you haven't been to a garbage dump, especially a fresh one, there's no way to convey the stench. The odor is thick and nauseating, like decadence and death; but there are also whiffs of extinction.

Needless to say, I dumped my brush and got out of there as fast as I could.

The average American creates four pounds of trash a day. Nationally, that's 600,000 tons every twenty-four hours, 210 million tons per year. Thirty percent of it gets reused or recycled, but the rest goes into garbage dumps, landfills, and our lakes, rivers, and oceans. With approximately 700,000 of us in Cowtown, we produce 1,400 tons of solid waste per day; after recycling, 1,000 tons go into "transfer stations." A thousand tons. Per day.

The Westside Transfer Station is pretty big, but it's going to take hundreds more just like it to keep us from drowning in our own garbage over the next generation. And when these dumps are full, they usually just get covered up. Eventually, many of them contaminate groundwater, aquifers, soil, and air. The Westside Transfer Station is within a half-mile of Mary's Creek to the north and two miles of South Mary's Creek, both of which feed into the Trinity. *Will our great-grandchildren's drinking water contain traces of the trash we set out on the curb today?*

My nine-year-old son's class is taking a field trip to the UTA planetarium this week. It will be educational and fun, but I have a suggestion: Make the transfer station the first stop.

As the kids take in the sights and smells, the teachers can emphasize the importance of cutting back, recycling, and composting. Then, when the kids get to the planetarium they'll understand better why space is so important—clearly we'll have to move out there someday.

We'll have to move to escape the planet we've poisoned and left virtually uninhabitable, eventually to become a future generation's myth of Atlantis, sinking below the garbage.

Unless, perhaps, our kids get the picture—sooner rather than later—and turn us around.

Politics (and Murder) Most Foul

Dissident Voice • *September 13, 2008*

From the listens and glimpses I got of the Republican National Convention a couple of weeks back, there were several efficacious speakers. Unfortunately, the theme that wove their speeches together and elicited the most spirited responses from the crowd was *ad hominem* assault. The Democratic National Convention, wisely or unwisely, called for unity and emphasized commonality. The Republican National Convention was simply another Neocon rendition of "it's us against them."

McCain often refers to himself as a "change" candidate, but his convention and subsequent campaign are obviously fashioned after the unrepentant wiles of Bush's "Boy Wonder," Karl Rove. Instead of attacking Barack Obama on the issues or his record, the Neocon spin machine is snidely ridiculing his background and personal style. It's clear they want to depict him as a suspicious, menacing "other" rather than a fellow American or another rational human being with different political beliefs. It is not their intent to constructively highlight policy differences or divergent political agendas. Their goal is to create fear and contempt in their constituents, so much so that it bleeds over into the ranks of undecided voters and the resultant hysteria transforms the political process into an ideological witch hunt.

Every time a presidential election cycle comes around these days, Republicans portray Democrats as godless, immoral and unpatriotic. Conservative blowhards like Rush Limbaugh disingenuously blast away at Democratic authenticity. Evangelical fear-mongers question and besmirch Democratic morality and motives. And propagandist scamps like Rove circulate fabricated dark secrets that hint at Democratic evils and general depravity (ask McCain—when he was running against Bush, the whispers concerned an illegitimate African American love child in South Carolina). The result is a spurious, wholesale denigration of Democratic candidates that leaves a large percentage of the American populace believing that if they don't vote Republican, God will abandon us, Satan will be nominated to the Supreme Court and Al Qaeda or Iran or Russia or China will be handed the proverbial keys to the kingdom.

In this same vein, the Republican convention clearly laid the groundwork for vilifying Barack Obama, and, as I watched, I kept waiting for Jim Adkisson to take the stage.

Perhaps you don't remember him.

Adkisson was the out-of-work, Tennessee truck-driver who recently decided "liberals should be killed because they were ruining the country." On July 28th, he walked into his former church (which he also felt had gotten too liberal) and started shooting folks who were gathered there for a children's musical. Two people were killed and six others were wounded. A longtime acquaintance later said Adkisson hated "blacks, gays and anyone different from him."

I sincerely doubt Adkisson came to hate liberals (et al) all by his lonesome while he was driving the byways and back roads of the American hinterland. In fact, if you retrieved his keys and went by the Knoxville Police impound and started up his truck, I bet you'd find his radio is still tuned to a channel that features the vitriol of hateful conservative talk show hosts.

Adkisson was hardly a lone gunman. He clearly had folks like Limbaugh and Glen Beck and Karl Rove whispering in his ear. And if you listen, you can still hear them: *Obama is different . . . Obama wants us to lose the war . . . Obama is the Antichrist . . . Obama called Sarah Palin a pig . . . Obama wants kindergarten kids to be taught sex education . . .*

When you characterize your opponent(s) as depraved, treacherous, evil and perverse, he becomes an enemy instead of an opponent. He becomes dangerous and destructive instead of just disagreeable or dissenting. This is the essence of Neocon politics. Once they convince their constituents that Democrats and liberals are diabolic and life, liberty and way-of life-threatening, it makes them easier to condemn, slander, sabotage, character-assassinate and ultimately—in Adkisson's case—murder. It's a Nazi tactic that Neocons ought be ashamed of, but they feel the ends (eight years of almost absolute, unaccountable power) justify the means.

Their entire modus operandi is based on the blatantly cynical supposition that the American public is perpetually irrational and the best way to get elected is to stoke our fears and prejudices.

The bad news is it's worked for at least two election cycles. The good news is the routine is starting to wear thin.

Eventually folks will get weary of the Neocons crying wolf, or Muslim or Antichrist. Let's just hope it's sooner rather than later.

Less Is More:
A Manifesto for Human Survival
Dissident Voice • *March 18, 2011*

Albert Einstein's IQ is estimated to have been around 160. The average American's IQ is ninety-eight. If an Einstein-like mind can be said to represent the upper stratus of individual intelligence in this country, please note that his IQ was not even double that of the current national average.

Based on intelligence alone, then, does any man, woman, magnate or CEO deserve to make more than twice as much money as the average rest of us based on how smart they are?

Jamaican sprinter Usain Bolt shattered the world record in the 100-meter dash by running it in 9.58 seconds. The average working adult in America probably runs the 100 meters in seventeen to twenty seconds and even the uncoordinated or mildly decrepit can probably manage it in thirty seconds. If Bolt can be used as an example of the highest level of coordination and speed that a human being can achieve, please note that his record-breaking time in the 100-meter dash probably isn't even three times faster than ours.

Based on speed or coordination alone, then, does any man, woman or athlete deserve to make three times as much money as one of us based on how fast they move?

A week has 168 hours in it. The average work week is forty hours. The practical maximum number of hours a person can work in a day for weeks and months at a time is probably sixteen hours. But let's say someone really motivated adds an extra eight hours to the 112-hour work week achieved at a sixteen-hour-a-day pace and consistently strings together 120-hour work weeks. Even if someone managed this incredible clip, he or she would only be working three times as much as one of us; so is there any way, based on the number of hours worked per week alone, anyone could deserve to make more than three times what the average worker makes in a week?

Some folks are stronger than others, to be sure; and some folks went to college. But the average professional football player isn't three times stronger than your average man and, I'm sorry, but the average college student isn't three times as educated as someone who just settled for a high school degree.

But let's say—hypothetically speaking—that we stumbled up against the ultimate wage or salary earner. Let's say he or she was two times smarter, three times faster, three times stronger, had a college degree and regularly worked 120 hours per week—even at that exaggerated pace and preposterous performance level, the basic math indicates that he or she would never deserve in excess of 162 times more than the average employee in the workplace. And yet we have corporate CEOs that earn five and ten times that.

Truth be told, our ultimate wage-earner does not exist and never will exist. And, arguably, there isn't a human being on this planet who's worth more than ten times the next, much less 100 times the next.

Sorry, again, but no one is that special. And no one is that in-dispensable.

Conceding these suppositions, then, compels us to answer two unpleasant but unavoidable questions.

First, regardless of how smart someone is or how hard he or she works, what kind of human being honestly believes they are 100 times more deserving than another?

Second, what kind of human being is actually driven to become the kind of human being who—in good conscience—receives 100 times more than another?

The former epitomizes what is worst in us as a species. The latter diminishes any hope we have for the future of our species.

The planet's resources are finite. The planet's ecosystems are imbalanced. Most of the planet's inhabitants are endangered. If our individual or collective definitions of success endanger other species or our own, jeopardize our habitats (specifically or generally) or deplete our natural resources, then we are not defining or achieving success. We are promulgating failure.

If the short-term "means" for a people's way of life are Capitalism, Materialism and/or greed in general, the long-term "ends" are death, destruction and doom. It can't be said any plainer. And we—as a culture and a species—pretend otherwise at our own rapidly approaching peril.

There's nothing wrong with being successful unless success is meted out in increments of extravagance or superfluity. There's nothing wrong with wanting to be successful unless you're measuring your own success in terms of extravagance or superfluity.

Our species will not survive as a pampered class or preferred tax bracket. The only abundance we should be encouraging is that of this very awareness. And any enlightened society should begin gauging individual worth in terms of the acknowledgment of this awareness and the steps we take to thwart the power and control of wealth and the wealthy.

Foreign Phallacy

Fort Worth Weekly • *March 4, 2009*

When a commercial for a male enhancement drug came on the other night while my family and I were watching television, my ten-year-old daughter said, "They shouldn't show that on TV."

Mildly dismayed, we asked her why.

"You know," she replied coyly.

When we prodded, she added that the advertised product made a man "bigger" and "stronger" in the bedroom.

When I was ten-years-old, I thought women got pregnant from kissing. My daughter already knows how babies are "made" and what options men can pursue to bolster their procreative capacities.

So much for the birds and bees speech.

I'm concerned—or at least feel like I should be—but I don't know what to do about it. There's no sense in humbugging or sanctimoniously speculating about what the world is coming to. My wife and I don't believe in sheltering our children, and we don't think they're better off home-schooled or forbidden to watch TV. There are some dangerous and disturbing things out there, but we don't believe in pretending otherwise. We think it's better for our kids to have some idea of what's going on rather than being naïve.

The fact that young kids know about penis enlargement and extra boom-boom in the bedroom is disconcerting, but I don't know why we were surprised. It's almost impossible for our kids not to notice, since the ads for (and news about) this stuff are everywhere.

Not long ago, Rush Limbaugh was busted at the Palm Beach International Airport for turning up with a bottle of Viagra without a prescription after a stag binge in the Dominican Republic.

During the recent presidential campaign, a brouhaha occurred when a McCain spokeswoman said birth control pills should be covered by health insurance just like erectile dysfunction treatments. McCain waffled, and Bill O'Reilly led the charge in his defense, claiming that drugs like Viagra address a medical condition and birth control pills do not. And then we learned that the CIA is doling out Viagra as part of our War on Terror.

It used to be that when we heard the acronym "IED" it referred to an "improvised explosive device," probably in Iraq. Now, in Afghanistan, the acronym signifies something else altogether. It stands for "incessant erectile dysfunction," and, apparently, it's the most successful tactic the CIA has found for winning the hearts and minds (and loins) of local Muslims—or at least, Muslim men.

Aging Afghan patriarchs with several wives are now our anxious allies. If a chieftain or patriarch has an erection lasting more than four hours, one assumes, they just add more wives or call their local CIA "mojo" huckster for a pass to the nearest U.S. military hospital.

It is said that the average man thinks about sex once every six or seven seconds, and I admit that there was a decade (or maybe two) where I probably fit that description. As a youngish forty-something, I still enjoy sex and don't need pharmaceutical props, but I'm glad the topic is no longer a 24/7 obsession. I'd like to think I've evolved or at least crossed a threshold that permits me to occupy my brain with more substantive matters. I suspect I am a better man (and certainly a better human being) for it.

And with my now multi-track mind I say that when my daughter finally comes of age, I hope that impotent blowhards will no longer be running the Republican Party, that birth control options for the young will be afforded the same political urgency as the fading libidos of their elders, and that our country will no longer be peddling "sexual steroids" to chauvinistic warlords as a way to gain allies.

Then perhaps my grandchildren will be able to watch television without being bombarded by the trials and tribulations of modern phallus worship.

The Ezekiel Flying Machine and the
Error Dynamic of Christian Aerodynamics

Dissident Voice • March 9, 2011

A few months back, I went to Pittsburgh, Texas, and got a good look at a replica of the Ezekiel Flying Machine. It took to the air a year before the Wright Brothers flew at Kitty Hawk, but only for 167 feet before crashing into a fence. The story is intriguing and noteworthy, but more as a cautionary tale than a serious scientific achievement.

In 1900, Reverend and lumber mill owner, Burrell Cannon decided he'd been called by God to build a flying machine. He'd studied the Book of Ezekiel for years and was captivated by its description of an "aircraft" that featured "a wheel in the middle of a wheel" by which "living creatures were lifted up from the earth." Cannon believed he could recreate the craft, so he sold his lumber mill in Pine and moved to Pittsburgh.

In Pittsburgh, he preached the Gospel and peddled his ideas for an aircraft designed straight from the Good Book. With the Almighty on his side, he sold $25,000 worth of stock and began construction.

Within two years, he completed a one-man, 26-foot flying machine that featured a light, tubular metal frame, an almost circular, fabric-covered flying-wing, a secondary lower wing and two pairs of wheels tucked below the wings. The outer wheels were eight feet in diameter and designed to taxi the craft up to take-off velocity; the inner wheels were paddle-operated and devised to drive the craft once it was aloft.

In mid-1902, one of Cannon's employees piloted the craft on its maiden flight. According to eyewitness reports, it picked up speed, left the ground, drifted in the air and began vibrating violently before its undercarriage collided with a wooden fence post as it passed over. Later that year the craft was destroyed by a storm while sitting on a flatbed train car on its way to the St. Louis World's Fair.

In the end, the Ezekiel Flying Machine was a marvel to behold, but Cannon's engineering was more beholden to the Holy Writ than the laws of gravity. Adhering to the wheel within a wheel concept made the craft a faithful clunker that was too heavy and unwieldy for practical flight.

We make this mistake all the time, even today. Creationists believe that God made human beings out of the dust of the ground, fashioning our oldest female ancestor as an afterthought and from one of the first human male's ribs. No sperm or egg. No DNA. No birth, infancy or adolescence. Just clay figurines animated and given a soul for good measure.

New or "Young" Earth theorists believe the Earth is no more than 7,000 to 10,000 years old and most of their data is based on counting up the generations in the Bible and adding them to the calculated number of generations since the Bible. No Homo erectus or Cro-Magnon steps in the process—just ready-made Homo sapiens that hit the ground begetting other Homo sapiens.

Both claims are more beholden to the Holy Writ than objective scientific analysis and they arguably require a suspension of critical thinking. For starters, the Bible was a latecomer on the scene. The Pyramid of Giza and the Epic of Gilgamesh predate it by millennia. Millions of folks were living in self-sustaining, fully-functioning communities long before Christ and Christianity ever appeared. And any serious student of the Bible and the history of the region knows that "Eden" narratives like the one found in Genesis and metaphors like the lord being a shepherd were borrowed from older cultures and pre-existing religions.

The Bible is an inspiring, poetic text but parts of it are hardly original and the parts that were original have been translated and re-interpreted more than once. Sacred, yes, holy, perhaps, but scientific—no.

If Reverend Cannon hadn't been hamstrung by the Bible, Texas might have been first in flight (the controllable, steerable, safely-landing kind). If the basis for our children's education was rooted in science instead of superstition, they might fare better against their overseas counterparts. If the Scriptures hadn't have indicated that Christians were meant to "have dominion" over "every living thing that moveth upon the earth," we probably wouldn't have such an absurd sense of entitlement and perhaps it wouldn't be so easy for us to continue marginalizing the rest of the natural world.

Religion isn't a bad thing unless it's applied badly.

Relying on religious beliefs to navigate gravity, education or science in general isn't just a bad idea; it's a bad application of faith.

As we stumble toward an uncertain future, do we really want to base our fate on faith?

Olympians Weren't Really
Representative of the U.S.

Fort Worth Star-Telegram • *September 3, 2012*

The London Olympic Games were a hit, and I enjoyed them. But I also found them disturbing.

On the one hand, I was proud of our athletes, their accomplishments and commitment, their courage and hard work.

On the other hand, however, I felt ashamed.

I felt ashamed and frustrated that, as incredibly and admirably as our athletes performed, they didn't represent us.

Not really.

If the gold-winning U.S. Women's Gymnastics team was truly representative of "us," they wouldn't even have medaled. These days we're not first, second or third in any rankings of real consequence, much less champions of good causes or fair outcomes.

And the last thing a team representing us would have been is united or working together, much less toward common goals. Petty dissension would have split their ranks. One or two of the Caucasian athletes would have demanded to see Gabby Douglas's birth certificate or accused Kyla Ross of being a Manchurian Candidate planted to sabotage the team's chances.

If the U.S. Men's 4 x 100M Freestyle Relay Swim Team was truly representative of us, it wouldn't have won silver in London. Bitterness and suspicion over accusations that Cullen Jones was only in the mix due to affirmative action probably would have crippled the team's efforts and made team members doubt and/or resent one another rather than strive collectively toward positive results.

If the U.S. Men's Diving Team was truly representative of us, David Boudia wouldn't have won gold in the 10-meter platform dive and Troy Dumais and Kristian Ipsen wouldn't have earned bronzes in the three-meter synchronized diving competition.

All three men were mentored by openly gay, HIV-positive Olympic diving legend, Greg Louganis. You and I discourage homosexuality and would never concede that gay folks have anything of worth, value or decency to convey to the young people in our communities, much less the sports they participate in.

We'd prefer diving into the nearest Chick-Fil-A to join the rest of the righteous, even if it meant losing.

Make no mistake.

The 2012 U.S. Olympic Team was not representative of us; *they were better than us.*

Team work. Trust. Shared sacrifice. Ethnic diversity. Sexual tolerance. Unity in the face of challenge, adversity, competition, difficulty. A wildly diverse group working together without suspicion or derision or someone holding up signs that say "God Hates Fags." Immigrants and the descendants of immigrants—champions assembled from the tired, poor and huddled masses (wretched refuse from a thousand teeming shores) sharing the toil and rewards without fear- and hate-mongers demanding to see their papers or making it more difficult for them to participate in the process because of the color of their skin.

I had to stop myself when I began feeling pangs of pride as our Olympians excelled in London, because I knew it was a pleasant mirage, an aberration.

My country no longer believes in greatness or teamwork. And the current levels of ignorance and close-mindedness that govern (and are encouraged by many of those who govern) this nation preclude it from golden accolades, particularly in terms of greatness and teamwork.

And what our athletes did in London was just a dream—an Olympic dream. A dream our athletes work hard toward but many of us don't even aspire to, much less condone.

While we sat there cheering our Olympians in London day after day, it never occurred to us that some of them represent the very same folks we're trying to take our country back from.

We're not "medaling" these days. We're meddling with the ideas and processes that made America great. And we're doing it for petty political points.

Unfortunately, there are no Olympic events for political expedience.

Road Rage

Dissident Voice • *April 24, 2010*

Okay, now I'm a traffic statistic.

On the way to work the other day I experienced a mild bout of road rage. I didn't get cut off and no one was creeping along in the fast lane. I simply saw one too many imbecilic bumper stickers.

I was practically indifferent to the old Corolla that's back windshield informed me that I shouldn't be fooled, the driver's treasure was in heaven. And I barely noticed the new Cadillac Escalade whose bumper sticker said "Not perfect, Just Forgiven."

Juxtaposed, I figured the driver of the Corolla had a better chance of maneuvering through the eye of a needle than the new Escalade owner, but they were both vying for real estate I didn't have much interest in. So I drove on unfazed.

Then, I passed a suburbia-optioned SUV with a bumper sticker that read "I love my carbon footprint." And the minivan ahead of it shifted into my lane and echoed the SUVs sentiment. It's window decal said "Global Warming is a lie."

Jeez, I thought. Why not just get a bumper sticker that says "I love chopping down rain forests" or "I heart human extinction"?

I know, I know. The jury's allegedly still out on theories like Global Warming, Climate Change and Evolution—but we've got indisputable proof of Jesus, God and the Easter Bunny, right?

I'm sorry.

I try to remain tactful and judicious, but what kind of buffoon comfortably publicizes such irresponsible nonsense? Global warming and climate change are not stand-alone phenomena concocted by scheming liberal scientists to deprive the leisure class of their unjust and proper spoils. They're happening in concert with hundreds and thousands of other alarming trends that all indicate that human beings are leaving detrimental "footprints" all over this planet. And our almost psychopathic missteps are not hard to track.

Unless you're woefully isolated or willfully ignorant, you see or hear about them every day. The Great Pacific Garbage Patch now has an Atlantic counterpart and scientists suspect there are others. Oceanic dead zones are multiplying, sea life is disappearing, coral reefs are dying, seawater is becoming more acidic and the migrations and territoriality of several telltale marine species have grown precarious and unpredictable. Our freshwater systems are being poisoned by urban run-off, toxic dumping, mining and drilling deposits, pesticide drift, acid rain and mercury. Our lands are being depleted by slash and burn farming, industrial agriculture, deforestation, desertification, soil salination and disappearing resources. And this planet's biological diversity is being decimated by systemic ecosystem erosion and toxicosis, habitat fragmentation, bioaccumulation, human overpopulation and plain old human greed and egotism. For our sins, however, our own bodies are slowly and incrementally becoming toxic soups of cadmium, lead, aluminum, benzene, formaldehyde, chlorine, acetone, mercury, benzopyrenes, nitrosamines, herbicides, household cleaners, etc., etc., etc.

Does the only hope for life on this planet have to be you and I eliminating our own species before it destroys all the others?

These crises are not cyclical.

We have seen the enemy and he is us, the guy looking at you in the mirror, the lady you see in your make-up compact, the karaoke stars on *American Idol*, the irrelevant jocks scoring touchdowns, dunking basketballs or sinking thirty-foot putts, the dim minstrels starring in summer blockbusters and the talk-show personalities proclaiming wisdoms or sharing recipes. We are onlookers and they are clowns. Their sole purpose is to keep us from getting too nervous about the human high-wire act that's transpiring in the big picture.

It was just a matter of time before the materialist dichotomy of artificial preservatives and planned obsolescence would make Capitalism obsolete. The high-wire act we're involved in is not death-defying; it's death inviting.

Life doesn't always go on. Especially when you leave idiots at the wheel, drunk with their own success, addicted to indulgence and blinded by their own cultural narcissism.

The bumper stickers I saw that morning inspired me to drive metaphorically, to speed up, but take my hands off the steering wheel, to keep moving forward faster and faster, but in no controlled, responsible direction. Would I run into the myth of global warming or trade paint-jobs with a beloved carbon imprint? Would I crash into someone who was more worried about treasure in heaven than sustainable life on earth or someone more content with being spiritually forgiven than existentially accountable?

Alas, the rage dissipated. We passed each other in our metal coffins on the way to our inconsequential vocations and all was right with my acquiescence.

There were clowns to watch on TV later and dire consequences to disregard.

A Whimpering Ixnay

Dissident Voice • *July 15, 2013*

Several Saturdays ago, a Mourning Dove woke me, its pseudo-forlorn coo complimented by the light patter of rain on my tent. It was the most peaceful moment of the day. I didn't want to get up, and I didn't have to. I was camping northeast of San Antonio.

When it rains at my house, it's mostly just something that happens outside my window or on my windshield. I rarely hear it or feel it. It's hardly an inconvenience, much less an interesting experience. But it was a big deal that morning because it hadn't rained in that region for a long while. The spring deluge that flooded areas of the Alamo City was welcome in the wild. It was life affirming, fecundating.

The previous week in the Metroplex, I'd checked the weather every day. Up until the Friday I snuck away it was all "No chance of rain," "10% chance of rain," etc. Perfect for camping. But the farther south I drove on State Hwy 281, the cloudier it became, and by Lampasas it was raining steady. Burnet was a torrent.

I was nonplussed. I was frustrated. I thought about getting a hotel. I even stopped at one and when I stepped out of my truck, the water in the parking lot was three inches deep.

Feet soaked, resolve shaken, I jogged into the hotel lobby to inquire about room pricing. I had planned for a little wilderness, but not rain. I would call an audible and simply camp the day after when the rain had stopped and things had dried out. I was ready to re-inhabit something approaching my comfort zone, but my weakness was fortuitously denied.

The lobby was busy. My fellow accommodation-seekers were all, in varying degrees, older, heavier and/or otherwise less disposed than me for a short stint outside their comfort zones, and I mildly cursed myself for the namby-pamby softie that I had become. What was that line from T. S. Elliott's "Hollow Men?"

This is the way the world ends: Not with a bang but a whimper.

I resolved not to truncate my short sojourn into the wild with a whimper.

I drove on out to the campsite, determined to make camp when the rain let up. It was never less than a steady sprinkle, but I pitched my tent and threw my gear in it. Then I stood a small pop-up tent shelter and placed my camping chair under it.

It poured some more.

It was too wet to build a fire, so I did head back to civilization for some ice and a bite to eat. It rained most of the night.

When the Mourning Dove woke me, I was amazed at how well I'd slept. Back home the rain would simply have been a mild nuisance, but there in the tent it was a small marvel. I laid on my back and listened to the doves and the rain and actually heard them for the first time in a long time. A lifetime ago. A time when I was maybe a little more alive and in touch with things that were more alive.

As the day wore on, the rain let up. I did a short hike. I dropped a line at what looked like a good fishing spot. I even swam a little.

Back at the camp, everything seemed greener. The land had been parched and the rain was a welcome drink. A squirrel from a nearby tree practically came up and gave me a high (or low) five.

It was great to be in a small way more in tune with nature than at odds with it. It was as close to approaching an Absolute Good as I had been in years. I was still something of an unseasoned interloper, but I was making an effort and it helped my perspective.

In a day or so I would be back in the city, shuffling papers, anchored to a desk, faking a living. All the silly, unnatural compromises most of us have to make to remain productive cogs in the machinery of our own physical and spiritual denigration.

In a few weeks I would forget what green in the wilderness after a rain looked like, but a Monsanto dye in one of our daily, unholy foodstuffs might approach it, and the giddy patter of rain or the song of a Mourning Dove—well, they would be etched in my memory for a month or two and then disperse like the dreams and honesty of youth.

Yes. Elliott was probably right. But I had a few more days to remain unspoiled or less spoiled in a place that was unspoiled or less spoiled, and for a time I would be less hollow.

The trick would be stringing together more less-hollow moments and experiences, perhaps crafting an existence preferable instead of just comfortable or bearable.

"Uno Calcetin" Says Vote for Pedro
Dissident Voice • *May 16, 2007*

In the summer of 1980, I got a job working for a landscaper. I was thirteen years old. I made $5.00 an hour.

The landscaper had five employees: me and four Mexican immigrants. Their English wasn't good and my Spanish was worse.

I was a light-skinned, clean-cut Gringo with blond hair and green eyes. The Mexicans were dark-skinned, slightly unkempt and fierce-looking. They wondered what I was doing there. They suspected I was a spy for our boss, who was also a Gringo.

The heat wave that year was as bad as anyone could remember. It was over 110 degrees every day and there we were, sweating over mowers, edgers and weed-eaters. We also trimmed shrubs and spread mulch and got on our hands and knees and picked weeds in flower beds.

We draped t-shirts over our heads and placed bandannas on our necks; by lunch our jeans were soaked all the way through with sweat. The sun bore down on us like an angry god.

Frequently, the edger or weed-eater I was operating would break down or run out of gas. I'd have to go find one of my co-workers. Sometimes I'd discover them huddled in the shade somewhere, sharing a watermelon or a big bottle of Gatorade. It took them awhile to figure out I was just trying to do my job, earn my keep and avoid a heat stroke. About a month into the summer, they were comfortable enough with me to tell me when they were taking a break, and we'd spend them together, sharing whatever we had.

There were no Port-O-Johns or ChemCans. If you needed to go to the bathroom, you had to improvise, sneak into a pool house restroom or walk to a convenience store. If you went to a convenience store, you had to buy something so no one pitched a fuss about your being there just to use the can.

On one occasion, I had a gastrointestinal emergency and couldn't find a pool bathroom or a convenience store. I had to duck off behind a giant hedge and wipe with a sweaty sock. One of my co-workers saw me and laughed, but he understood. They all understood. It didn't stop them from calling me "*uno calcetín*" for the rest of the day, but anything for a smile in the oppressive heat made the day go faster.

At one point that summer, I wore a bathing suit under my jeans and sneaked in a swim at an apartment pool. I tried to get my co-workers to join me, but they refused. I pressed them after the swim and the oldest one educated me. "You are like one of them," he said, in broken English. "You look like *el jefe* . . . if other *Gringos* or *el jefe de las casas* catches me . . . or one like me swim in pool, we lose job."

I didn't swim again.

The landscaper transported us on the back of his flatbed truck, crowded in with the mowers, edgers and weed-eaters. The best part of the day was heading home on the flatbed, sitting next to a mower and feeling the almost cool swoosh of open air rushing against our skin and drying our sweat-soaked shirts.

One afternoon, as we drove past Six Flags Over Texas on Interstate 30, it occurred to me that one of my classmates was probably on the "Shockwave" right then (or getting doused by a splash of cool water on the "Log Ride") and I felt ashamed. My co-workers didn't even know what Six Flags was, much less that their flag was one of the six, and I knew that they were simply looking forward to flipping on the window A/C in the four-walled shack that our boss picked them up and dropped them off at every day. I knew I would be going back to school soon and they would still be sitting on the flatbed, watching the heat waves glide across the freeway.

From then on, when a man or woman stared at my co-workers as they passed us, and then did a double-take when they saw me, I glared back accusingly, challenging them, judging them for judging. It was the closest the Mexicans and I ever came to solidarity. But it was enough.

I think about my landscaping co-workers a lot when I read about border walls, sting deportations and new immigration laws. If more Mexican immigrants were lighter-complected and had blond hair and green or blue eyes, I can't help but think it would be tougher for us to judge them, dismiss them or pretend they're really that much different from us.

We sure like hearing ourselves referred to as the "Land of Opportunity" but, unfortunately, we're trying real hard not to live up to this moniker. Bigotry prevails and we've got to find somebody (besides ourselves) to blame for our problems.

Mexican immigrants make an easy political *pinata*.

Conformity:
A Destructive Communal Neurosis
Dissident Voice • *September 5, 2008*

The other day one of my sons wanted to do something just because most of the other kids were doing it. I ceremoniously imparted to him wisdom that has been carefully passed down from generation to generation in our family. "Just because everyone else jumps off a bridge," I said, "doesn't mean you have to, does it?"

He looked at me like I pulled a vacuous, parental crutch out of my ear rather than making an intelligent comment. And of course he was right.

First, wanting to do something or wear something or join in something that most of the other kids are doing, wearing or joining is not as dangerous or life-threatening as jumping off a bridge. Second, how many of us really want our kids to be different than the rest?

Don't answer that question before really thinking about it.

Let's be honest. How many of us really want our kids to be different?

If you have even half-objectively surveyed the surrounding offices or cubicles at work lately you know the answer, but you don't want to admit it.

Go ahead. Tell the truth.

How much upward mobility do nonconformists enjoy at your place of business? What's their employment expectancy?

They don't spend enough time yucking it up on the golf course or posing at Starbucks. They're not reverent or obsequious enough to grovel or flatter their way into the big promotions. They don't worry enough about vanquishing the next guy (or gal) much less screwing over the easy marks.

Make no mistake. Conformity is a control mechanism that keeps the United Corporations of America sputtering along, unhealthy of course, but productive enough to keep the shareholders comfy. We may not be headed in the right direction, but our lemming-esque locomotion is a marvel of multi-media-induced coordination, social engineering and perpetual, material-assuaged surrender.

We pay lots of lip service to daring to be different and not caring what other people think; but when it comes right down to it, we're despicable hypocrites. If we don't look the right way and say the right things, the wretchedly superficial social circles we covet entry into are inevitably closed to us. If we don't go along to get along, vocational success eludes our grasp. If we don't parrot the proper patriotic slogans and dimly accept all those maliciously crafted and incessantly repeated talking points, we're deemed suspicious or subversive and dismissed by the hapless majority who believe they're in the know. Heck, if we didn't vote for Bush a few years back, we were practically traitors.

This is the world we live in. "Jumping off a bridge" used to be considered aberrant behavior, but now it's the norm. Metaphorically speaking, we jump off bridges every day, because it's exactly what everyone else is doing, it's what's expected of us and we don't have the courage to deviate from the norm.

If you don't want your kids jumping off bridges like everyone else, lead by example. Stop agreeing when you disagree. Stop acquiescing when you're right and they're wrong. Stop cowering before corrupt or illegitimate powers. Stop trusting news sources that bank on you being an ignorant, manipulable cretin. Stop giving credence to dissenting "authorities" propped up by gainful factions with ulterior motives. Stop simply believing what you want to believe and spend some time discerning what's believable. Stop preferring short-term gratification to long-term health and sustenance. And stop letting yourself off easy.

We achieved the current catalogue of impending dooms as a reckless species, a careless people and as irresponsible individuals. To thwart our societal plunge, the buck has to stop with you, every one you know and every one you ever knew. Everyone everywhere.

Conformity is the currency of dilapidation. It compromises every aspect of our politics, our lifestyles, our worship and our wellbeing. If, as Einstein put it, insanity is "doing the same thing over and over and expecting different results," then conformity is at least a little psychotic if not outright insane.

Isn't it time we acknowledged our psychosis and dealt with it?

Untuck your shirt. Defy instead of defer. Speak truth to panderers.

Until we stop jumping off bridges, our advice to our children is just effective reverse psychology. And the last thing we should be able to stomach is them ending up like us.

The Grapes of Ignorance

OpEdNews • February 20, 2010

Almost every time I visit the lobby of my bank, the flat-screen TV in the waiting area is tuned to the Fox News Channel. One day, I asked a bank representative why. She said that too many patrons found CNN offensive.

A couple of days later, I was at a mom-and-pop diner and the TV was tuned to CNN. As I sat picking at my food, a customer in the booth next to me mumbled that he would take his chicken fried steak to go unless they changed the channel.

Wow, I thought. *What's happening to us?*

Was ignorance always a matter of principle? Or was it something we embraced over the last ten years or so?

The current extent to which close-mindedness permeates every aspect of the American conversation is as shocking as it is sad. Tunnel vision passes for awareness and obtuseness is acclaimed as virtue. Open minds are openly discouraged, taunted and endangered.

For all the unprecedented access we have to information, news outlets and divergent viewpoints, we are less informed than perhaps ever before and much more easily manipulated. We fell for WMDs in Iraq, "Mission Accomplished," the myth of the liberal media, "Too big to fail, "Death Panels," etc., etc. We were duped by lie after lie and mocked by sham after sham.

If a shill for our viewpoint says it, we believe it. If a shill for the opposing viewpoint says it, we refuse to believe it. And, if evidence arises to challenge our position on an issue or disprove it, we simply cry conspiracy or recuse ourselves from reality.

In chapter fourteen of *The Grapes of Wrath*, John Steinbeck says the thing that the powers that be must bomb to preserve themselves is downtrodden folks' cognitive shift from the individual "I" perspective to a collective "we" plurality. As long as disenfranchised folks are struggling alone, the world is aright for the ruling class. But the minute two or three or a thousand disenfranchised folks get together and begin struggling in unison, then those "who hate change and fear revolution" have a problem. To manage the downtrodden, Steinbeck says, you must keep them apart and "make them hate, fear and suspect each other."

Sound familiar?

If you listen to the partisan mouthpieces on talk radio or tune in to the broadcasting arms of our two major political parties on TV, it should. By fostering animosity and ignorance they render us easier to control. By demonizing or dehumanizing their opponents, they promote hate, fear and suspicion.

Essentially, both sides play their part. When liberals behave condescendingly towards conservatives, the powers that be nod approvingly. When conservatives call progressives communists or Nazis, the ruling class tap dances gleefully around their cash registers. Divisiveness diverts our attention from the facts and polarization paralyzes our efforts towards reform.

Steinbeck was commenting on the potential power that could be harnessed through solidarity. But the disenfranchised never acted on these instructions purposefully or methodically, especially in a long-term sense. And whatever gains were made here and there were subsequently thwarted or lost.

The powers that be, however, took note. Today, they no longer have to worry about bombing us. It's easier just to place microphones or cameras in front of rabid ideologues and let them ragebait us into a WWE Smackdown frenzy.

Know this. The values of Liberals are closer to those of the Christian Coalition than the ruling class. And the Tea Partiers have more in common with Progressives than the corporate elite.

If we had any sense, we'd be more inclined to brave the bombs of the powers that be than quibble over their scraps.

State-sanctioned Martyrdom
for God and Capitalism
Dissident Voice • August 5, 2009

When I read about the recent deaths of Edward and Joan Downes, I remembered a few lines from *Romeo and Juliet*. Before Romeo drinks his "dram of poison" to join Juliet, he says:

> *O, here*
> *Will I set up my everlasting rest*
> *And shake the yoke of inauspicious stars*
> *From this world-wearied flesh. Eyes, look your last!*
> *Arms, take your last embrace! And, lips, O you*
> *The doors of breath, seal with a righteous kiss*
> *A dateless bargain to engrossing death!*

Edward, a knighted, eighty-five-year-old British music conductor, had serious health problems and was almost blind and deaf. Joan, a seventy-four-year-old former dancer, choreographer and TV producer, had cancer.

Rather than suffer under the "yoke of inauspicious stars" or perish at the whim of their increasingly decrepit, "world-wearied flesh," the Downes' chose to pass on together with shared grace, dignity and courage. Unfortunately, they had to travel to Switzerland to do it.

Assisted suicide and euthanasia are banned in Great Britain as they are in most places here in the United States. The healthy majority generally believes it knows what's best for the rest, and the chorus of misery that emanates from many of the terminally ill and the grotesquely suffering ultimately gets drowned out by a din of Christian rhetoric and ludicrous moral posturing.

In *Romeo and Juliet*, the abrupt, hardly weighed suicides of the protagonists are considered romantic. Almost 500 years later, the peaceful, deliberate passing of the Downes—a couple that had been together fifty-four-years—is frowned on by many as selfish, immoral and damning.

Some say it's a direct violation of God's law. Others quote Corinthians 6:19, 20 (KJV): "Know ye not that your body is a temple of the Holy Ghost, which is in you, which ye have of God, and ye are not your own." They believe God has proprietary rights and we mortal chattel dare not question His plans, even after His arguably having been asleep at the wheel for the last couple of millennia.

I couldn't disagree with them more. Their stance suggests that terminally ill folks should voluntarily play Job, regardless of the pain and anguish that accompanies these often horrendous and hopeless deaths.

I think what God allowed to happen to Job was a sin and worse than a sin. The Book of Job reads like a bet between two sadistic guards at a Nazi concentration camp. If two human beings of sound mind choose to die quietly, bravely, and determine their time, their own end, to alleviate their sufferings or agony or induce their own demise before they've lost all semblance of their lives or themselves—if they decide they've played Job long enough, how can we fault them for cheating their torturers and how can any good god punish them for refusing to fulfill the wager?

Religion is not all that demands this abridgment of free will, this prohibition of peaceful oblivion. America used to be at the forefront of compassionate ideas. Now, we lag behind, hobbled by short-sighted Conservatism and wide-eyed profit-mongers. The powers that be have no problem with us killing ourselves slowly with cigarettes or alcohol or their unnecessary drugs or the synthetic poisons they peddle or indirectly place in our food, air and water supplies. Each and every one of us is a captive consumer and even after we can no longer eat, drink or defecate their poisons on our own and we've forgotten who we are or were, they can still make money off us rotting away under hospice care or in a nursing home.

Who are we to take matters in our own hands? Who are we to circumvent the burgeoning assisted "living" industry?

I'd like to think we're human beings. I'd like to think we would be treated humanely. Unfortunately, only the states of Oregon and Washington have "Death with Dignity" laws in place.

Here in Texas, regardless of how identity-erasing, volition-robbing, life-transmogrifying, excruciating, needless or pointless a dying person's wasting away may be, he or she is expected to grin and bear it.

What we want doesn't matter. Even after there's hardly anything left of us, they still place the cross, the yoke and the burden on our shoulders. It's a state-sanctioned martyrdom for God and Capitalism.

Healthy Debate

Fort Worth Weekly • *July 29, 2009*

Earlier this month my wife had a surgical procedure performed at a fairly new hospital in Fort Worth. The doctor was remarkable, the nurses and staff were great, and every step of the process was made as simple as possible.

Since my wife has good insurance, she didn't have to save for months to afford the procedure or wait until the last minute and stagger into an emergency room. There was no crowd and no waiting room filled with the bloody, dazed, or urgently infirm. She got red-carpet treatment. The hospital even offered valet parking in the patient drop-off area.

I was grateful, but it also made me uncomfortable. It was almost like a country club.

My wife and I are barely on the middle side of middle class. The only reason she received this superb treatment is that her employer offers an outstanding benefit package.

Without her job, we might have wound up at a cheap clinic or over at a public hospital where the closest you get to valet is an ambulance.

The other day, as I was watching my youngest son play soccer, I looked out at all the boys and wondered what kind of treatment they would receive if a serious ailment arose. What if their parents didn't have good insurance? What if their parents didn't make enough money?

Who in good conscience could stand up and say one person and his or her children deserve better medical care than another? *Who would do that?*

That's easy.

The good ol' U.S. of A.

That's how our healthcare system is currently run, right now, every day.

If you have good insurance, you get VIP treatment and valet parking. If you have bad insurance, they get to you as soon as possible, but the cost is often more debilitating than the injury you get treated for. If you have no insurance, you get there the best way you can, and they treat you when they can.

My mom's father was involved in one of the forward campaigns of D-Day. He got shot in the upper part of his thigh and lay on the battlefield, probably thinking he was going to die. But he didn't. A German combat medic treated his wound. My grandfather didn't speak German, and I don't know if the German medic spoke English. But I doubt he asked my grandfather if he had money for the procedure or good insurance so the Third Reich could be reimbursed for his life-saving treatment. My grandfather—the enemy—was wounded. And the German medic simply did his job, regardless of uniform, nationality, class, etc.

American combat medics are instructed to do the same. In fact, such treatment is mandated by the Geneva Convention. But it doesn't apply to American civilians in peacetime, except in dire emergencies. If you have a pre-existing condition, most insurance companies will refuse to cover it. If you want to keep your insurance premiums reasonable, insurance companies simply stick you with savings-demolishing deductibles. If you work for small companies that offer health insurance and one of your co-workers gets cancer and requires expensive long-term treatment, the company's insurance carrier raises the entire company's premiums until it can no longer afford to offer the benefit.

Arguably, my grandfather received better and fairer treatment on the battlefield from the enemy than many Americans get from their own healthcare system today. And make no mistake: The medical industry and the insurance companies that discriminately dole out access to the medical wares too often treat the poor and disenfranchised with less respect than they would afford a (well-insured) enemy.

I don't blame the doctors or nurses or surgeons. I blame the system. Any system that offers better or worse treatment for my child or any of his soccer teammates because they have more or less money or better or worse insurance is wrong, unconscionable, and evil.

The *Declaration of Independence* clearly states that we are all endowed with certain unalienable rights, among these "life, liberty, and the pursuit of happiness." The right of "life" is made alienable by our healthcare system. So think real hard before you laud the status quo or oppose a major overhaul in the inflated, bankrupting nightmare that serious medical treatment amounts to for millions of people in this country. If you don't have much money or insurance and you get sick, you'll find yourself tossed onto the health insurance industry's class battlefield. And there might not be any Nazis around to save you.

Oh, for a Reality-based President
Fort Worth Weekly • July 3, 2007

On a September evening in 1956, Marian Keech, a middle-aged woman living in the American Midwest, claimed she received a message from a planet called Clarion, saying that the world would be destroyed by a catastrophic flood on Dec. 21.

Keech said the message also informed her that several flying saucers from Clarion would come and rescue her and those close to her before the deluge.

Mrs. Keech's revelation attracted a small group of ardent followers. They quit their jobs, gave away their money, and withdrew from friends and family; some left their spouses. And then they waited.

On the morning of Dec. 20, Mrs. Keech said that she had received another communication from Clarion: She and her followers would be picked up at midnight, and they should make sure there was no metal on their persons. Her followers dutifully removed metallic clasps, zippers, and buttons from their clothing.

When midnight came and went, the group became anxious. By 4 a.m., they were sitting in stunned silence.

Then, just when the gravity of their mistake had begun to sink in, Mrs. Keech received a third message: The rescue saucers had been canceled because the planetary cataclysm had been diverted by the unwavering faith of her group. Mrs. Keech and her followers rejoiced and began spreading the good news.

To outside observers, Mrs. Keech's followers appear to have been incredibly gullible. But consider the alternative: If Mrs. Keech was a fraud, then they had uprooted their lives for nothing and, perhaps, worse than nothing, a lie. But if they had saved the world, they were part of a miracle. Their sacrifices of familial relations and worldly possessions had saved the rest of us.

Mrs. Keech's followers remind me of contemporary Bush loyalists. During the 2004 presidential campaign, Bush once said his base was comprised of the "haves and the have-mores." Today his base is made up of the "ignores and the ignore-mores"—folks who have invested so much of their energy, enthusiasm and integrity in supporting Bush that it is now too hard to admit that they were lied to, have defended lies, and have politically embodied a lie for the last seven years. The evidence is all around them, but they refuse to face it.

Support for the Bush administration began tailing off after the Abu Ghraib scandal and the Valerie Plame leak. After investigations determined that there was no pre-war connection between Saddam Hussein and al Qaeda and no WMDs in Iraq (just as Plame's husband Joseph Wilson had originally insisted), Bush's approval ratings nose-dived and never recovered. Since then staunch "Bushies" have no longer enjoyed the pseudo-cover of righteousness and patriotism once afforded them by an obsequious, muzzled press corps. The rapid public opinion shift resulted in substantial election losses for their party. Suddenly, in a country where "W" decals once adorned every other car and truck on the road, it was hard to find any.

Now, as the war (or, better said, our occupation) in Iraq drags on, it has become painfully clear that the entire fiasco was based on lies. Big lies, compounded by dozens of ludicrous, outrageous smaller ones—on facts spun, truths distorted: *Mission accomplished! The insurgency in Iraq is in its last throes. They hate us for our freedom.* And so on.

Amazingly, Bush retains the support of millions of diehard followers, still repeating the party line from planet Clarion. If Saddam didn't have WMDs, *well . . . we know he was trying to get them. If al Qaeda wasn't in Iraq under Saddam, uhhh . . . well, they're there now, and they must be stopped.*

It's just the liberal media twisting things around.

Freedom isn't free.

Like Mrs. Keech's group, loyal Bushies seem capable of believing anything that will allow them to postpone admitting they were wrong. Facing the facts would require an admission of guilt, of the blood on their hands. It's easier to keep drinking the poison Kool-Aid than to own up to the horrors that their blind allegiance has helped bring to the world.

Unlike Mrs. Keech's followers, however, Bush loyalists have no chance for a "happy" ending. The war in Iraq will not be won. And our conduct there will remain a blotch on our national self-esteem for decades. In the end, the unfortunate soldiers who lost their lives, limbs, buddies, or peace of mind in Iraq will have done so for nothing.

I wish flying saucers from Clarion would come down and make our mistakes in Iraq disappear. But it's not going to happen. This time, unwavering faith has doomed us to disgrace. And the sooner we accept it, the sooner the healing will begin.

We Have Bigger
Abortive Problems than Abortion

Dissident Voice • *May 17, 2011*

For as long as I can remember, I have been pro-choice. Even at an early age, it seemed to me that impregnation had for centuries been an effective means of controlling women, putting (and keeping) them in their "place," restricting their potential and limiting their existential options.

Motherhood is a wonderful thing, a noble venture and perhaps the most important task a human being can perform; but it's not the only wonderful, noble or important achievement that women are capable of.

Birth control was a revolution and the resulting, newfound reproductive sovereignty gave women more freedom and yes, more choices. That is why I have always been pro-choice.

Regardless of how much religious zealots, pro-lifers or chauvinists of the old patriarchal order try to make abortion the central issue of the day or the next presidential election, it's simply neither and, to be honest, it's not even the most immoral or destructive abortive process that affects our daily lives.

A thought is a living thing. It begins as an infinitesimally small electrical impulse. Coordinating synapses. Connective neurons.

If it's allowed to thrive, it can become a way of seeing, a path to knowledge or a means of survival. If it's allowed to live and breathe in the life of the mind, it can become an idea or an ideal and perhaps even evolve into a revelation.

Today, unfortunately, too many critical thoughts are willfully terminated before they are begotten. Our minds are pregnant with perceptions and understanding, but too many of our conceptions don't survive to fruition. Too many of our intellectual offspring never see the light of day.

They say an abortion of the reproductive variety is performed every thirty-seconds in America. I suggest to you that an abortion of the intellectual variety is perpetrated a million times every thirty-seconds.

I know what you're thinking

You're thinking I'm not going to pull this metaphor off. But at least you're thinking. An intellectual concept is in play.

You and I are consummating a thought process, but you want to make sure the cerebration is healthy or acceptable to you before you allow it into your world. So be it.

Most opponents of reproductive abortion are religious. They believe reproductive abortion takes a life, prevents a life or generally interferes with God's original commandment (the first instructions He ever gave us): "Be fruitful and multiply."

Their claims may be correct or at least exhibit correctness, but their reasoning is stunted and hypocritical. Through conditioned naivete or mandated ignorance, the thought processes relative to this issue were aborted, lest progenitors be stuck with unwanted notions or demanding insights that they were not prepared to nurture.

Reproductive abortion does block and prevent a life and interfere with God's first commandment. But anyone whose thought processes are not institutionally or piously aborted knows that birth control pills and condoms also block or prevent lives and interfere with God's first instruction.

So if you're on the pill or using condoms, sponges, diaphragms, etc., you can't condemn abortion. All birth control measures are part and parcel of the same perceived sin. And, if we're being honest, we shouldn't be waiting till we've finished high school or college or until we've put a mortgage down on our first house either. God didn't command us to just be fruitful when it was convenient.

The cognitive impulse you and I have pursued is now a growing thought process. *Is it kicking yet?*

If we can stave off our conditioned, critical thought-aborting tendencies toward ignorance, we can agree that birth control isn't a bad thing. It can obviously be unpleasant and it may often be abused, but thought control is arguably worse.

We've been reproductively fruitful. The shape of our planet is a testament to that.

It's time to be intellectually fruitful and multiply our critical thought processes, embrace independent cognition and nurture practicable, mortal insights instead of deferring to antiquated, default supernatural commandments.

Congratulations!

We may just have created a new consciousness.

Reconverting the De-converts:
A New Modus Operandi for the Church
Dissident Voice • November 26, 2010

In the November 23 edition of *Christianity Today* (an online "Magazine of Evangelical Conviction"), Drew Dyck bemoaned the current trend of "leavers" or young doubters who are abandoning the church at an alarming rate. In 1990, eight percent of all Americans claimed "no religion." By 2008 it was fifteen-percent overall and twenty-two-percent among young people. Dyck pointed out that seventy-three-percent of the "no religion" respondents came from religious homes and sixty-six-percent could be considered "de-converts." Church leaders are obviously concerned about apostasy and are currently debating possible causes and solutions.

I am not a "de-convert" or a "leaver." Christianity never spoke to me or I was simply too obtuse or skeptical to hear the call. But I did have more respect for the institution a decade or so ago, and I think I could make some useful suggestions for those trying to protect or revitalize the flock. I have no ulterior motive and this is not an attempt to undermine The Word in America.

First, the church needs to stop falling for false messiahs. Prior to George W. Bush's ascendance to the U.S. presidency in 2000, he claimed God had contacted him and told him to run. The Bush Campaign shrewdly played upon the fears and consternation generated by the approaching millennium change, Y2K, etc., and used them to its advantage. Half the country was mildly fearful that the world would be ending (or at least attended church a little more regularly to play it safe) and Bush captured the White House by classifying himself as a born-again, evangelical Christian, virtually ordaining himself the Chosen One to stave off the Apocalypse.

It was a Karl Rove special that worked to perfection.

A vote for the Democrats was practically a pledge to the Devil and, as posterity will eventually note, the Moral Majority cast their lot with one of the least Christian leaders in the history of the United States. President Bush lied us into a war, pandered to the wealthy instead of protecting the weak and de-criminalized torture so American operatives could brazenly commit war crimes heretofore only associated with unholy outfits like the KGB or the Khemer Rouge.

What would Jesus Christ have done?

None of the above.

He didn't speak to George W. Bush and He wouldn't have voted for him.

When the church hitched its wagon to a cleverly disguised heathen, its image was tarnished by shabby association and people's faith in The Word suffered. In the future, Christians would be well served to remember the First Amendment-mandated separation of church and state for their own sake. In this case, it might have preserved some of their following.

Second, Christianity today needs to concede the lessons of history and science's place in history. The theory of evolution may still not be 100 percent, but it's getting there and resisting the obvious simply prolongs the presence of egg on the church's face. In the history of the Word (as its proponents interpret it) versus Big Scientific Blasphemies, the Church is winless. Galileo was right. Columbus was right. Darwin will be proven right. Do what you always do and simply incorporate new knowledge into the doctrine. Say Adam was made of clay, but through a type of biological claymation rather than offhand clay-shaping. Say God's crafting of Adam was a process, not a spontaneous production. And similar rational approaches should be encouraged towards global warming and/or climate change. The church should never openly invite environmental calamities on the scale of a Revelations narrative. Encourage a Christianity that is less anti-intellectual and your message will become more reasonable and inclusive.

Third, stop letting pedophiles, morons, and the Republican

Party claim they represent you. Address molestation charges directly. Don't simply transfer the culprits. Punish them and strip them of their religious offices. The best damage control is not denial. It's justice.

Disavow shameless, self-promoting imbeciles like Sarah Palin. Christian representatives may be fallible and imperfect, but there's no reason to add stupid and petty to the list. When shameless scamps hold themselves up as exemplars of your faith, they cheapen it. Call them out and denounce their charade.

Realize that Republicans are no more Christian than Democrats and challenge yourself with this question: Would Jesus have been on the side of Big Oil, Big Insurance, Big Pharma, or Big Business?

Jesus Christ is speaking to you now, so loudly that even I can hear Him. Four divinely throated "Nays" and zero "Yeas." The pretense of Republican righteousness is duly exposed.

Your savior was not a money-changer, a Capitalist or a fear-monger, and He wouldn't have stood with them or their like in the subjugation of His people. His was a message of love, compassion and transcendence. Juxtapose that message with the Republican messages of Rush Limbaugh and Glen Beck.

Non-Believers like me certainly enjoy the company of "leavers" and the "de-Converted" in our existential abyss, but I don't feel they'd be too hard to re-convert or bring back into the proverbial fold. You've just got to stop insulting their intelligence, misappropriating their faith and diminishing their hopes for humanity

Goebbels Would Have Been Proud

Dissident Voice • *April 27, 2010*

For the past month or two, I've been watching too much TV. Especially movies on cable. It's been a regrettable lapse, but not entirely wasted. With my fingertips on the remote-controlled pulse of America, I learned one interesting thing: Nixon is making a comeback.

I was only seven-years-old when President Nixon left office, but I remember it pretty well. Even for a boy, Nixon was a suspicious character, the kind you wouldn't accept a ride from. Unfortunately, the country took the ride twice, and, shortly into his second term, Nixon resigned in disgrace.

To be fair, my childhood recollections were later colored by Hunter S. Thompson's *Fear and Loathing on the Campaign Trail in '72*. It was a compelling hatchet job of "Tricky Dick" and the sinister atmosphere of the Nixon era, and whatever suspicions I had harbored towards the man early on were clearly magnified by Thompson's obvious contempt for him.

That being said, two movies I saw during my cable lapse altered my perception. The first was *Frost-Nixon*. It was an excellent film that explored the implications of the first televised "gotcha" moment of an American president, but it was done very even-handedly and actor Frank Langella brilliantly captured Nixon's stunted, yet genuine humanity. I sincerely felt for Nixon after the movie, even if I still didn't agree with his politics.

The second movie I watched was *Watchmen*. In it members of a group of disbanded superheroes come together to save the world from nuclear Armageddon. It takes place in the early 80s and President Nixon is in his fourth term.

It's a crazy idea, no doubt, but it got me to thinking. What could have happened to make it possible for Nixon to serve four terms?

In the movie it isn't explained. In the graphic novel of the same name, I learned Nixon was still in office because the utilization of superheroes allowed the United States to win the Vietnam War. This alternate reality, however far-fetched, was intriguing, and it immediately spurred further thought.

If Nixon had won the Vietnam War would it have saved his administration?

The answer is possibly yes, but only because Rush Limbaugh and *Fox News* weren't around yet. If Limbaugh and *Fox News* had been around in the early 70s, Nixon would never have been forced to resign in the first place, regardless of the outcome in Vietnam.

With the Limbaugh/*Fox* spin machinery in place, the Watergate break-in would have been no more damning to the GOP than the Bush Administration's outing of CIA agent Valerie Plame or conservative activist James O'Keefe's alleged tampering with the phone lines of Louisiana Senator Mary Landrieau. The My Lai massacre in Vietnam would have been no more damaging than Blackwater's Fallujah Massacre in Iraq, and the invasion of Cambodia—well, it wouldn't have been anymore questionable or unethical as our invasion of Iraq.

The murders at Kent State would have been no more unpopular for Nixon as the failures in addressing Hurricane Katrina were for Bush. And musical artists like Bob Dylan or Crosby, Stills, Nash and Young would have been threatened, blacklisted and publicly disavowed for even criticizing President Nixon just like the Dixie Chicks were after they criticized President Bush.

In fact, if Rush Limbaugh and *Fox News* had been around in the early 50s, Senator Joe McCarthy's Senate Permanent Subcommittee on Investigations might have burgeoned into a Department of Homeland Security, Senator Joe McCarthy probably would have run for president and iconic newsman Edward R. Murrow would have been forced to resign just like Dan Rather.

The crimes of the Nixon years were minuscule compared to

those of Bush-Cheney Administration and, in retrospect, it's increasingly obvious that Nixon stalwarts Dick Cheney and Donald Rumsfeld clearly learned from Nixon's lack of media cover. Neither Cheney nor Rumsfeld considered Nixon's mistakes as errors, but simply unfortunate press clippings. With the full force of a national propaganda network behind it, the Bush-Cheney Administration became an unstoppable steamroller until the Iraq War dragged on too long and liberal and unbiased media outlets started exposing the lies behind the absence of WMDs in Iraq.

If you watch *Fox News* or listen to Rush Limbaugh and process what they're selling, you realize it's just anti-Democratic filler wrapped around Republican talking points. *Fox News* is a broadcasting subsidiary of the Republican Party and Rush Limbaugh is the archangel of an exasperated legion of backwards, misinformed cranks who are thrilled to hear someone justify their innate fears, bigotry and general xenophobia.

Limbaugh and *Fox News* knowingly and implicitly work to create and sustain conservative suspicion and hatefulness and incite irrational but effective phobias and paranoia to determine local, state and national elections. *Fox News* calls itself "Fair and Balanced," but to describe the work of Fox or Limbaugh as either is like the Third Reich labeling itself peaceful and inclusive. The latter was a fascist regime that killed millions. The formers comprise a fascist regimen that misinforms millions.

Goebbels would have been proud.

American Male Sports Obsession in Perspective

Aledo Community News • *May 20, 2011*

When *City Slickers* came out twenty years ago, it was obviously no *Citizen Kane*. It had a few funny one-liners and Jack Palance's screen outlaw persona was finally rehabilitated, but, beyond that, it was just a late thirty-something's feel-good dither on lukewarm masculinity at the end of the 20ᵗʰ century. But there was some dialogue I've never forgotten.

It comes in the early middle of the movie when the lone female "city slicker" asks her male counterparts why baseball is so important to them. Phil Berquist (played by Daniel Stern) responds: "When I was about eighteen and my dad and I couldn't communicate about anything at all, we could still talk about baseball. Now that was real."

The moment is mildly poignant, first, because it's obvious Phil loved his father deeply and baseball provided them a "real" forum to communicate through. Second, because even though Phil and his dad loved each other, the only way they could relate was through the clichéd, statistical vernacular of a wholly inconsequential children's game played by grown men.

Berquist's statement—the pathetic nature of which is never really considered or expounded upon—is still ludicrously germane to any discussion of American manhood today, because sports frame the American male psyche.

Generally speaking, sports define early male ego and often establish a basic though flawed criterion for prepubescent, pubescent and young adult male worthiness in terms of socialization, popularity and, yes, even procreation. Sports establish a cultural norm that men have a hard time giving up and/or trying not to live up to even years after they're physically able to do so. That's where collegiate and professional sports come in.

Collegiate and professional sports allow grown men to continue participating in the defining norm of their youth peripherally, passionately extolling the virtues of the spectacle and, on some level, competing vicariously through each generation that follows in their footsteps. This is why most elderly men know more about Mickey Mantle than McCarthyism. This is why most middle-aged men know more about Michael Jordan than the Iran-Contra Scandal.

Plainly put, professional and collegiate sports are a colossal drain on the American male (and female—but male in particular) attention span and they keep him from seriously focusing on dozens of events and developments that more directly and eminently affect his existence. And the little background and understanding that too many American men do have regarding these phenomena is largely gathered cursorily through slanted cable news or belligerent talk radio. It is a dire cultural and societal problem.

The Texas Rangers professional baseball team has a wildly successful ticket sales campaign that says "Get your Texas Rangers tickets now and watch history being made." Except history isn't being made by the Texas Rangers baseball squad, especially not in any real, relevant, or broadly meaningful respect. And it's not being made by the Dallas Cowboys, the Dallas Mavericks or anyone racing out at Texas Motor Speedway either.

Real history is not made by grown-ups who play children's games or folks obsessed with Hot Wheels for adults. It's made by serious people addressing serious problems. It's made by protestors and visionaries. It's made by leaders and inventors. It's made by heroes and contrarians.

History is not reported in the sports pages and you won't find it on a baseball diamond or football gridiron or under a basketball net. That's why American men, in particular, must be called out. Their self-indulgent, superficial dalliances with college and professional sports now start in August and preoccupy them all year round. Football. Nibs of hockey. Basketball. World Series. More football. Bowl games. Baseball training camps. March Madness, Baseball, NFL draft, more baseball, NFL training camps. Then tailgate and repeat.

If an insidious presence in this country had actually investigated, researched and formulated a long-term societal scheme to limit meaningful male participation in and broad awareness of the most profound cultural and political processes and events of our time (or any time), I'm not sure they could have come up with a better idea than American sports. They are now scheduled so perfectly that they keep a daunting percentage of the male population from ever having to think real hard about much else besides sports. They go from one season to another, following overlapping seasons concurrently. Men buy season tickets. They join fantasy leagues. They keep statistics. They participate in office game and tournament pools. They bet with bookies. Their obsession with college and professional sports is so profound that college coaches make more money than tenured professors and professional children's-game stars make more in one contest than good elementary, junior high or high school teachers make in an entire year (including summer school duty).

Think about that for a second.

When sports are more real and more valuable to us than our children's educations, aren't we lost, gone astray and courting cultural disaster?

Isn't it about time we men put down our pom-poms? Don't we have more important stats to keep track of? Shouldn't we concern ourselves with more pressing issues?

History is being made these days, but mostly without our involvement and certainly without our consent. And the teams that are winning "most definitely" want to keep it that way.

Texas Monstrosity

Dissident Voice • *June 22, 2016*

Two years ago, on June 23, 2014, Dallas resident Charles Robert Moore drove to his hometown of Grand Saline, Texas and parked his car in a Dollar General parking lot on East Garland Street. He lingered there momentarily and then placed a foam mat on the ground. He knelt down on the mat, poured gasoline over his head and lit a match. He immediately burst into flames.

As Moore stood up and began to scream, two men rushed over and extinguished the blaze. He was transported to Parkland Hospital, but succumbed to his burns later that day.

By all accounts, Charles Robert Moore was a man of conscience and conviction. As a former Methodist minister in Austin, Moore participated in over 100 protests against the death penalty and once went on a hunger strike to protest discriminatory language in the literature of the United Methodist Church.

He traveled in India, Africa and the Middle East and was not afraid to challenge his beliefs. He was also steadfastly committed to defending the rights and beliefs of others. As one colleague put it, "If you were ever on the side of powerlessness, if you were ever on the margins yourself and looking for someone to help you, Charles was the person."

In his retirement—at an age when most folks relaxed and contented themselves with sitting back and simply enjoying the time they had left—Moore was still mindful of injustice. He thought back to his youth in East Texas. He lamented the discrimination and persecution that African Americans there had experienced at the hands of their white neighbors and wondered if he had done enough about it.

He was haunted by this question.

Though Moore's existence was characterized by courageous stances and an unwavering adherence to the principles of righteous opposition, Moore was troubled by the possibility of his own adolescent apathy and/or inaction—what most of us would consider a forgivable dalliance of youth. He wanted to bring attention to the atrocities that African Americans in his community suffered and the continued disempowerment and marginalization that they endure to the present day.

After Charles Robert Moore killed himself, his relatives found a note that conveyed the sense of urgency he felt regarding the issue he died for:

> I would much prefer to go on living and enjoy my beloved wife and grandchildren and others, but I have come to believe that only my self-immolation will get the attention of anybody and perhaps inspire some to higher service.

Moore's hometown newspaper's response to his act was to describe him as a troubled old man. The *Tyler Morning Telegraph* reported his self-immolation under a headline that read "Madman or Martyr? Retired minister sets self on fire, dies."

The story of Moore's self-immolation made the *Telegraph*, the *Longview News-Journal*, the *Dallas Morning News*, the *Washington Post* and a few others; but his death did not draw widespread, serious news coverage or attract substantial attention to the history and issues he was disturbed by.

In Moore's own words:

> Many African Americans were lynched around here, probably some in Grand Saline; hanged, decapitated and burned, some while still alive. The vision of them haunts me greatly. So, at this late date, I have decided to join them by giving my body to be burned, with love in my heart not only for them but also for the perpetrators of such horror.

Over four dozen African Americans have been burned at the stake in Texas, and the majority of these tortured souls met their fiery end in East Texas. The crimes that Moore was concerned about are still being ignored, and the regimen of domestic terrorism these atrocities represent is still hardly being discussed, much less acknowledged or addressed.

There is something evil about living oblivious to these monstrosities. There is something monstrous about Texans and Texas communities who condone this ignorance.

What's Wrong in Texas?

Dissident Voice • *January 18, 2014*

The first thing you notice about Texas in 2014 is there are some new sheriffs in town and they're not male or Caucasian. Electorally speaking, they're female and/or Hispanic. Women and Hispanics may not have been beating down the door for the role because they were busy as bees, making inroads, building careers, bringing home the bacon, raising kids, etc., etc. But a nefarious assemblage commonly referred to as the ruling class (or Good Ol' Boys Club) has kicked the proverbial beehive one too many times and now it's likely to pay.

Truth be told, it's been a long time coming.

For all the bitching and moaning about the Mexican-American element in Texas, white conservative male tightwads couldn't stomach paving their driveways without the cheap labor it provides, even if their fair-haired grandkids are being challenged in terms of aptitude and usefulness by the average day laborer's sons and daughters every day. And for all the Texas white male's drawled braggadocio about treating women with the respect they deserve, conservative white male politicians have doubled down on treating women like second-class sex objects that can't be trusted with decisions about their reproductive rights. Breast implants are fine, but a brain functioning beyond or despite the institutional chauvinism that was implanted in young Texas women's brains over the last century or so—no, that's not acceptable.

Unfortunately—for conservative white males—they hardly have a grasp on acceptability, tolerance or social justice. The last time I thumbed through a book on Texas history, I'm pretty sure I saw that white males didn't build this state alone or in a vacuum.

They had women, wives, sisters and daughters right alongside them all the way. And lest we forget, of the estimated 189 men who died at the Alamo, only six were native Texans: their last names were Abamillo, Badillo, Espalier, Esparza, Fuentes, and Navatwo. And the signatories of the *Texas Declaration of Independence?* Only two were native Texans. Their last names were Navarro and Ruiz.

The days of Anglo-male entitlement are about as fresh and relevant as Colonel Sanders, and he (pardon the pun) kicked the bucket just before the "Miracle on Ice" in 1980. For decades conservative white guys have fancied themselves champions of all things Texan and the progenitors of all the cures to the maladies that ail Texas citizens. But the fact is, the conservative white guy has become the chief malady that ails Texas.

Thanks to conservative white males, Texas is home to the highest percentage of uninsured folks in the nation, enjoys the highest carbon emissions, is first in high school drop-out rates, first in lowest voter turn-out, is the biggest producer of hazardous waste and, thanks to a pasty-white, testosterone-slicked fortune grab, Andrew's County is now home to a nuclear waste dump designed to house radioactive refuse from up to thirty-seven other states.

And the owner of that new 14,000-acre nuclear waste dump in West Texas?

You guessed it.

A conservative white guy from Dallas (Harold Simmons, recently deceased) who was last presidential election's third-largest Republican donor and the largest contributor to Karl Rove's conservative super-PAC, American Crossroads.

But I digress.

We must also, of course, pat conservative, white male backs for a few things.

We're not dead last or first worst in everything. There are twenty states with lower average IQs, nine states fatter and six states that rank lower in child well-being.

I am a white guy and I know white guys are used to telling folks how to vote, who to vote for to be right with Baby Jesus and who to vote against to keep us from being overrun by Kindle-toting Socialists who want to put fruit and granola in our high school cafeterias and literacy and science in our classrooms—so I won't tell you who to cast a ballot for in 2014. But I do have a useful historical note.

The year 2014 is an important anniversary for any Texan who isn't male or white.

White male conservatives in Texas kept women from exercising full suffrage until 1918 and minorities from voting without hindrance or intimidation until the Voting Rights Act of 1965. Not small feats, to be sure, but 2014 marks the 60th anniversaries of Hispanics and women gaining another arguably equally important right under American law, that being the full and unfettered exercise of due process.

Prior to the 1954 U.S. Supreme Court decision in *Hernandez v. Texas*, Hispanics were entitled to a so-called fair trial, but not to a jury that had any other Hispanics, much less other persons of color or women. Justice was almost invariably meted out by white men, white juries and white, almost exclusively male judges. Women and minorities weren't entitled to an actual jury of their peers and nothing was done about it for the first 118 years of the republic/state's existence.

Conservative white males had a big head start and it's no wonder that they still harbor a hefty sense of entitlement around these parts.

But it also explains a lot about what's wrong.

We Are the Beasts

Fort Worth Weekly • *April 14, 2010*

In many ways, Hunter Layland was like any other freshman boy in the Metroplex. He played football, spent time with his friends, and tried to adapt to high school. But unlike most young people learning the ropes in our communities, Hunter didn't have much luck. He'd been in a car wreck as a toddler, and it left him with facial scarring and hearing problems. At Cleburne High School, he was constantly made fun of. Some of his schoolmates even went so far as to say that if they looked like him, they would kill themselves.

On September 31, 2009, at 6:35 a.m., Hunter did exactly that.

Over the last few months, I've thought a lot about Hunter and some of the kids who got bullied when I was in school. Some of them had it pretty rough, but most of us hardly even noticed or cared. I think about the scorn and derision they endured and how, even though I usually wasn't party to it, I certainly didn't do much to prevent it. I was too concerned with being cool or popular or simply deferring to the bigger kids.

I remember the victims' names and faces. I even remember what was said to them and about them. They were targets of ignorance, stupidity, and sheer meanness. They were often teased unmercifully no matter what they did. And, like Layland, their attempts to placate their tormentors only made things worse.

Looking back, I can't help but despise myself a little for not doing something. I could say it wasn't any of my business or my fight. But that doesn't help. What happened to some of these kids should have been everybody's business. We were all to blame.

As I get older and re-examine the events of my life in broader perspective, it's not always the things I did that give me painful pause. It's often the things I didn't do, like not speaking up when I should've or not standing up when others were being pushed down.

This summer will mark the 25th anniversary of my high school graduation. Out of my class of about eighty-five kids, only two have died—and both committed suicide. One killed himself while we were still in school, the other a few years ago. I hardly knew the former and certainly wasn't a friend. I knew the latter well enough, but we had our differences. I don't remember either of them being obvious marks for bullies, but they didn't have it easy either. And when I read that another kid at my old high school committed suicide this last fall, I couldn't help but think of them. And Hunter Layland.

I don't know how some of the kids we mistreated had the fortitude to keep coming to school. The slights, the name-calling, the trip-ups. There wasn't a lot of room to breathe. And there certainly wasn't any room to be different.

My classmates who were the most accomplished tormentors back then are normal folks today, happy, complacent, and church-going. *Did they finally achieve enough popularity or a strong enough sense of superiority to erase the need to bully? When they get down on their knees to pray at night, do they beg forgiveness for what they did to kids like Hunter?*

In my experience, our victims usually don't attend class reunions, and, if they do, they seldom betray any hard feelings. *Did that which didn't kill them make them stronger?*

What is it in so many of us that craves superiority, that requires us to put down others to feel better about ourselves?

We seem to need victims, pariahs—collective or individual otherness that we can rally against or look down upon. In fact, it often seems like that's when we're most comfortable.

I hope Hunter is at peace now, in a place where scars and misfortune don't make him the target of human knavery. I'd like to think he didn't die in vain, but the news indicates otherwise. As long as folks are still showing up at town hall meetings with guns or threatening people whose color, belief system, or appearance they don't like, then the bullies are still at it. And we're still not stopping them.

Overthrowing the Overthrowers
Dissident Voice • *May 16, 2009*

On April 17th, Dorrie O'Brien, a local conservative activist and spokeswoman for a political advocacy group called American Congress for Truth, told a Metroplex Republican Women's organization that most if not all Muslim-Americans were involved in terrorist operations within and without U.S. borders. On May 4th, as guest speaker for the North Tarrant Republican Club, O'Brien reiterated her claim, bemoaning the "Islamization" of America and claiming that Muslim-Americans were trying overthrow our country.

Also at the May 4th engagement, the North Tarrant Republicans allowed thirty-year Tarrant County Medical Examiner (and Muslim-American) Nizam Peerwani to rebut O'Brien's claims, but O'Brien had exited the premises before Peerwani spoke.

O'Brien's one-sided dialogue on this issue unfortunately typifies the prevailing tendencies of American conservatism and Republican politics over the last eight years or so. There's the world according to them, wherein they are patriotic, morally superior and righteous, their positions unassailable; and then there's world according to the rest of us, but our political, philosophical and social divergences are simply wrong, un-American, godless, evil, etc. This is why so many of Bush's press conferences and town hall meetings were strictly populated with conservative disciples who gushed with weepy-eyed pride no matter what Bush said. His handlers wanted a controlled, homogeneous crowd where objections could not disrupt his talking points.

In the event that contentious views were aired, the Bush Administration made the progenitors of such impieties pay. If you were a general who disagreed with the Bush Administration's Iraq war strategy, you were forced to retire. If you were the chief contracting officer for the U.S. Army Corps of Engineers and you charged that major Pentagon officials exercised questionable favoritism towards Halliburton in regards to military contracts, you got demoted (*See* Bunny Greenhouse.). If you were a CIA agent whose spouse refuted the Bush Administration's claim that Saddam Hussein possessed WMDs, you got outed (*See* Valerie Plame.). If you were a U.S. Attorney investigating Republican "super-lobbyists" like Jack Abramoff, you got dismissed (*See* Frederick A. Black.).

Clearly, the "my way or the highway" approach that Republicans passed off as a higher principle during their recent tenure evidenced an unsettling strain of Fascism, a la Dick Cheney, Donald Rumsfeld, Karl Rove, Rush Limbaugh, et al. The problem is, however, that too many folks in the Red tent still don't see it for what it was. And this is where O'Brien could really help.

As a member of an American congress for "truth," O'Brien could encourage her conservative cohorts to actively seek exactly that. If America is on the verge of being "overthrown," it's not happening at the hands of Muslim-Americans. It's happening at the hands of the misguided conservatives and Republicans.

Muslim-Americans didn't manipulate the conservative-leaning U. S. Supreme Court to abridge our electoral process. The Republicans did. And behind closed doors they'll tell you the ends justified the means.

Muslim-Americans didn't suspend habeas corpus, banish due process or trample over our 4th, 5th and 6th Amendment rights. The Bush White House did, and it didn't bother them one whit. As Bush himself put it, the U.S. Constitution is "just a goddamned piece of paper."

Muslim-Americans didn't push us into repeatedly violating our own laws against torture, much less Common Article 3 of the Geneva Convention. Cheney, Rumsfeld and Condi Rice did. And they're still trying to justify it.

Muslim-Americans didn't pat Big Oil or the Big 3 automakers on the back and say keep on cranking out those gas-guzzlers because the Carlisle Group goes on forever and the party never ends. Conservatives and Republicans did. And their unrepentant mantra is still *"Drill, Baby, Drill!"*

Muslim-Americans didn't try to violate our separation between church and state, deny global warming, illegally wiretap our conversations, ban the teaching of evolution, vilify poor people, demonize gays, marginalize dissenting voices or deregulate our economy until it dove to lows we haven't seen since the Great Depression. Republicans and conservatives accomplished these feats all the while dressed in their Sunday-go-to-meetin' best.

If O'Brien is really an advocate of "truth," I'd like her to think real hard and honestly answer the following question: *If Muslim-Americans really wanted to overthrow or undermine the United States of America, is there any way they could possibly be as prolific in this task as conservatives, Republicans and the Bush Administration were?*

Inexplicable, Amusing,
Accidental Wonders Make My Day

Fort Worth Star-Telegram • *June 22, 2009*

On June 10, at 5:35 p.m., I was sitting at a red light at the Bryant Irvin Road bridge that crosses Interstate 20. My car was facing north, and I was third in line.

If you frequent this intersection, you know the red light lasts forever. Your hair gets grayer, your kids grow an inch and the needle gauging the $2.59-a-gallon gasoline droops toward "E" as you wonder when work will pick up so you can afford to have a doctor look at the spots on your shoulders that you suspect might be skin cancer.

You also have time to ponder various news items of the day, like theoretical mathematicians discovering that the Earth might slam into Venus in 3.5 billion years and another conservative wack job is suspected of gunning down another innocent, this time Holocaust Museum security guard Stephen Tyrone Johns.

I was sitting at the light irritated by the wait and fretting over gun-toting conservatives when a tire whipped through the intersection, rolling west to east. The crossing was empty except for that tire and it was moving along like it was nobody's business. The traffic lights were red in every direction and drivers all around were annoyed by the lull, indignant because the lights indicated it was nobody's turn to go; and there goes this tire rolling by on a rusty rim, no vehicle or driver attached.

Had it bounced out of the back of somebody's truck?

Had it fallen off a car?

The tire ignored the red light and managed not to hit or be hit by the cars around it, and there it was, breaking the rules, defying convention, making a go of it, now passing in front of the Saltgrass

Steakhouse and headed down the access road toward Hulen Mall.

As the crossing traffic light changed, the vehicle cater-corner on my left took off, catching the renegade radial and avoiding it as they went.

I couldn't stop watching. I wondered how far it would get.

When my light turned green, I wanted to turn east and follow the tire, but I was in the middle lane. I wondered if there were any red-light cameras at that intersection. If there were, I wondered if they had snapped pictures of the tire, and, if so, what some red-light-violation video clerk would think. No license, no seat belt, just an inanimate configuration of rubber and steel doing what it was supposed to do. Roll.

It changed my whole day. It was inexplicable, amusing and poetic—an accidental wonder. I hadn't seen one in a while, and it gave me pause.

Every day isn't the same. The grind just deadens us to the subtle differences and intermittent marvels that occur moment to moment.

We might be a quintessence of dust subject to every manner of pettiness and foolishness, but every speck has its day. God, Allah, Buddha, Elvis or wily chance interjects and the self-imposed, collective drudgery of contemporary existence is swept aside, and we're treated to a glimpse of something contrariwise. And it's an absolute good.

Ads for temporary impotence cures will continue to pay for conservative talk-radio blowhards to incite hatred and violence and innocent people will continue to die; but appeals to hate and fear are as impotent as those who heed them, and this sad frenzy will pass. Someday our world may end, but better at the whim of gravity than the greed of Big Oil or Big Energy or our species run amok.

We're going to atrophy at red lights and ponder the world and our regrets, but also our hopes and the enchanting ironies that sustain us. It's not much, but it's enough.

Life would be much less tolerable without the small anomalies that confound Big Brother and the randomness that defies our best-laid plans.

Teenage Wasteland More Informed
Than Elderly Whine
Dissident Voice • March 22, 2013

On July 1, 2007, Austria reduced its voting age to sixteen. I was forty-years-old at the time and found the move both fascinating and unsettling.

On the one hand, even though anyone under the age of 18 in this country is considered a juvenile and usually can only be prosecuted in a juvenile court, every state lists exceptions for trying teenagers as adults. And if you're old enough to be prosecuted as an adult, wouldn't it be appropriate for you to have a say in who determines what laws affect you?

Many American sixteen-year-olds are already driving, carrying auto insurance, getting tickets and working part-time jobs. They pay income taxes, Social Security, Medicare, etc.—is it outrageous to suggest they might deserve a role in our political process?

On the other hand, I was sixteen, thirty-years ago—and when I wasn't fantasizing about Jennifer Beals in *Flashdance* or Rebecca DeMornay in *Risky Business*—I was courting premature hearing loss under the incessant audio influence of Rush, Triumph, Van Halen, Motley Crue, the Scorpions, etc. The closest I came to being interested in politics was slam-dancing to tunes off The Clash's *Combat Rock*.

That being said, I wasn't racist or homophobic, I understood evolution and I never questioned the notion that women deserved absolute sovereignty over their own bodies and reproductive processes. I was arguably as qualified as most of the adults voting back then (Case in point: In 1980 they elected a B-movie hack—who had matter-of-factly rolled over on his own friends and colleagues during the McCarthy hearings—to the highest office in the land!) and I arguably would have been more qualified than at least half of the voting-age populace today.

I bring all this up because last week I was sitting in a Fort Worth eatery, enjoying lunch, when two white-haired, male sixty- or seventy-somethings slid into the booth directly in front of me and began parroting conservative radio talking points. Then, the one with his back to me chalked up Obama's re-election and the current campaigns designed to reduce gun violence to matriarchal hysterics.

"Women," he said. "They're responsible for this whole mess."

I paused in mid-mastication.

"People on hormones should not be allowed to vote," he continued.

The old chauvinist said it too loud and with too much certainty, and my proximity to him suddenly filled me with dread. I suspected that any minute a member of the fairer sex within earshot might vociferously re-acquaint him with reality, but the gods of misogyny protected him for that moment. His hormonal "inferiors" were spread elsewhere around the restaurant.

In a bank lobby a few days later, another seventy-something turned away from live coverage of former Navy SEAL Chris Kyle's funeral at Cowboy Stadium and informed me and the rest of the bank customers waiting for their turn at the teller counter that Kyle was assassinated because he knew something about the mistakes made at the U.S. Embassy in Benghazi. He implied that Eddie Ray Routh was an Obama operative and said that "Kyle was killed to keep the truth from coming out."

I shook my head.

The average age for the *Fox News'* viewership is sixty-five. The average age of Rush Limbaugh's daily audience is sixty-seven. This isn't a coincidence.

I have long railed against teen television and cable programming (MTV, MTV2, MTV Jams, etc.) that serves up mind-flushing gems like *Jersey Shore*, *MTV Cribs*, *Punk 'd*, *Buck Wild*, etc., etc. It panders to the lowest teenage denominator. But as much as I detest it, it's practically Baby Einstein compared to the programming on *Fox News* the last couple of years and Rush Limbaugh throughout his entire Republican reign. And these conservative media outlets in particular (and in general) create, confirm and comfort a strain of American imbecility that's 20 million times more dangerous than Snookie-Bieber programming. Because the millions who consume it go out and vote.

Even in a pubescent, 80s blur of Jennifer Beals, Michelle Pfieffer, David Lee Roth, and Joe Strummer, I absorbed, acknowledged and—for the most part—observed the prerequisite adage instructing us to respect our elders. There were less of them around then and longevity was a rare feat. Today, longevity is not a rare accomplishment. Advances in medical technology make it commonplace and achieving the rank of elder no longer requires special wit or wisdom or exceptional health.

I believe my elders should be treated with dignity and respect, but some of their collective attempts to vote us back to the 1950s are a little disconcerting and I'm alarmed by their general intolerance, bigotry, and xenophobia.

Their vulnerability to misinformation channels makes them no more informed than their grandchildren and their intractability doesn't protect the future of our youth—it restricts it.

I think young American men and women aged sixteen to eighteen deserve the option to address their elderly counterparts at the ballot box.

December 7th:
A Shameful White Texan Anniversary
Dissident Voice, December 7, 2016

The last reported instance of white Texans burning an African American at the stake occurred eighty-three years ago today, December 7, 1933, near a black neighborhood in Kountze, Texas.

On Saturday, December 2, a thirty-year-old white woman named Nellie Williams Brockman left her and her husband's farm and headed to a department store in Kountze by truck. Somewhere along the way she ran into trouble and was apparently shot. They found her body next to the truck and both the vehicle and her corpse were partially burned.

After Brockman's body was discovered, a few folks claimed they had seen a shotgun-carrying black man head into the woods not far from where the crime was committed. Local law enforcement officials mounted an intensive search for the suspect, utilizing platoons of armed volunteers and keen bloodhounds, but turned up nothing.

A few days into the manhunt, the Kountze Police Department became interested in an African American man named David Gregory. According to the *San Antonio Express*, Gregory, a preacher's son, only became a suspect after a anonymous "tip": "Cloaking their investigation in secrecy, officers said the tip was of such nature that to divulge it would greatly jeopardize chances of apprehending the fugitive."

The *Galveston Daily News* indicated that the tip came after Gregory was suspected and that it's source was one of the suspect's aunt. Whatever the case, when Gregory learned that he was a suspect, he disappeared and at least six African American men (including Gregory's brother) were arrested in an attempt to determine his location. The *News* suggested that the informer placed Gregory at an African American church in the small community of Voth (now part of the northwest section of Beaumont, just east of U.S. Hwy 96 and the Pine Island Bayou).

On December 7, Hardin County Sheriff Miles D. Jordan, Sr., Deputy Sheriff Ralph B. Chance, Jefferson County Sheriff W.W. "Bill" Richardson and Deputy Sheriff Homer French headed to Voth and discovered Gregory at the described church, apparently concealed in the belfry. When they asked him to come down he refused and "flourished" a pistol (not a shotgun, the weapon the black suspect was reported carrying near the crime scene). Deputy Chance subsequently felled Gregory with a shotgun blast, the buckshot tearing into Gregory's face and neck and rendering him unconscious.

Sheriff Jordan and the others took custody of Gregory and immediately transported him to a Beaumont Hospital. He was in critical condition and received emergency treatment, but the doctors indicated that he probably wouldn't survive till morning.

Sheriff Jordan had hoped Gregory would regain consciousness so the investigation could record his statement, but less than two hours after their arrival at the hospital, word was received that a mob had formed in Kountze and was headed towards Beaumont. Hospital authorities subsequently conveyed their discomfort with harboring a suspect that could put the facility at risk and Sheriff Jordan calculated that their chances at keeping Gregory from the mob were slim, in or outside the hospital.

Sheriff Jordan and the others snuck Gregory down a back elevator and placed him in Jordan's vehicle. Jordan, Richardson and French (in two separate cars) eluded the mob and drove toward Vidor (seven miles east of Beaumont), planning to double-back and take Gregory to a hospital in Port Arthur (thirty miles farther south). Gregory never regained consciousness and died not long after the sheriff's car crossed into Orange County. Sheriff Richardson and Deputy French returned to Beaumont and Jordan pressed on.

As a mob was out and in force, Sheriff Jordan was not exactly sure what to do with Gregory's body. He considered a return to Beaumont unwise, so he turned and drove to Silsbee (twenty-three miles north/northwest). At Silsbee another mob had assembled and the local undertaker, fearing trouble, refused to accept Gregory's remains. Members of the Silsbee mob confronted the sheriff, but he convinced them to let Gregory's body remain in his custody.

With limited options and operating under the assumption that the Kountze mob was still in Beaumont, Sheriff Jordan headed back west. When he entered the Kountze community, an imposing throng of white men crowded in front of his vehicle. As reported in the *Corsicana Daily Sun*, Jordan described the scene thusly:

> It was a sea of faces of silent but grimly determined men.
> I guess I might have got part of the way through by running over and killing a bunch of white men. I wasn't going to do that to save a dead negro who was guilty of a most revolting crime.

As Sheriff Jordan would later put it, he was "one against four hundred," and the four hundred seized Gregory's corpse and tied it to the back of an automobile. A fifty-car parade of white men then dragged the body around Kountze for close to an hour, so long that a large bonfire that had been lit to incinerate Gregory burned out.

Denied a fire, the mob (according to the *Orange Leader* newspaper of Orange, Texas) "mutilated the body horribly in a savage demonstration of its spirit" and then re-fastened it to a car and "bounced" the body through the African American section of Kountze, reportedly screaming "Nigger for breakfast!" (several accounts—including that of the *Houston Chronicle*—suggest Gregory's heart was cut out and a 1972 account indicated it was nailed to a tree on Main Street)

Members of the mob then delivered the mangled corpse to the front doorstep of Gregory's mother, whom they summoned.

Mrs. Gregory appeared and succinctly denied the mob her anticipated hysterics. She glanced over what was left of her dead son and said "You've done it right, white folks," and went back inside.

The white folks retrieved the hide-less grotesquery and dragged it to a new bonfire that had been built in a vacant lot not far from Gregory's home. The conflagration was constructed of fencing removed from neighboring African American yards and as Gregory's remains cooked, some members of the mob drank coffee and ate sandwiches. Several others started towards the jailhouse to lynch some of the other black men in custody. Sheriff Jordan met the vigilantes out front and informed them that the facility was well-protected and that they would have to go through him and his men first, so the mob reconsidered or just ran out of steam.

The following morning, African Americans who passed by the smoking embers of the lynching pyre were reportedly called over to "see what happened to David Gregory." Some Texas newspapers included a photo of Gregory's remains smoldering in their December 8 reporting.

By afternoon, the white citizens of Kountze had grown concerned about the possibility of African American retaliation or an "uprising," so Kountze law enforcement personnel went through the black neighborhoods confiscating guns and knives. They stored the confiscated items at a local store until white trepidation passed.

Several years after the Gregory lynching, a local white man confessed to the murder of Nellie Williams Brockman on his deathbed.

It is important to recall this history because folks that look like me—white folks—got away with it. Folks who burned dozens of black men at the stake. Folks who committed racial expulsions and perpetrated wholesale massacres.

Today, we approve of voter suppression and summary execution and elect governors who hunt at places with names like "Niggerhead Ranch." We have the upper hand and we maintain it assiduously. We feel it's our birthright. And as our privilege and pseudo-superiority are increasingly questioned and challenged, we claim we're being put upon, or wrongfully vilified. We consider criticism of our entitlement an act of subversion and sedition.

White fragility has its roots in white monstrosity. And since we white folks have never had to acknowledge much less atone for our catalogue of inhumanities here in Texas—particularly involving persons of color—ignorance must prevail. We feel our entire way of life depends on it.

TAKSing Our Patience

Fort Worth Weekly • *November 15, 2006*

Used to be there were only two things sure in this life: death and taxes. Now there are three sure things: death, taxes, and TAKS (Texas Assessment of Knowledge and Skills) tests. I was never a fan of the first two, but neither is as inestimably pointless as the latter.

Originally implemented to hold Texas schools accountable for the public funds they receive, TAKS testing has taken over classrooms, requiring teachers to spend most of their time preparing our kids for testing rather than really teaching or inspiring them. Essentially, our children are being subjected to a cookie-cutter aptitude test that measures parroted knowledge instead of practical know-how, bland memorization instead of meaningful information, and factoid inculcation instead of intellect. Of course this opinion clearly emanates from a non-standardized, un-assessed, un-TAKS'ed Texas mind, but I think the entire program completely misses the proverbial forest for the trees.

Albert Einstein, whose teachers thought he was retarded in grade school (probably because he daydreamed too much and stared out too many windows), noted that "Imagination is more important than knowledge."

Let me repeat that.

Imagination is more important than knowledge.

Since we recently observed the fifth anniversary of the 9/11 attacks, it's worth noting that this sentiment is echoed in the final findings of the 9/11 Commission. The mistakes made by the Bush administration and our intelligence community were not attributed to a lack of knowledge or diligence. They were blamed on a "lack of imagination."

The TAKS does not test imagination. It tests transitory knowledge that our children absorb through rote instruction. It doesn't test a student's capacity for critical or original insight, creative cognition, or independent conceptualization. In other words, it's a great test for conventionally bright kids who are destined to become Capitalist lackeys primed for a slow but potentially lucrative climb up through the bureaucratic entrails of corporate America. Simply put, it prepares incurious, pliable vessels to listlessly consume prepackaged instruction and successfully regurgitate it in a prescribed, measurable manner. It doesn't measure intelligence, but rather intellectual etiquette.

Now, I can see why intellectual etiquette appeals to the more conservative, conformist aspects of our national identity. But it will not benefit us in the long run, and it will not keep us on top of the global political food chain. What's always made this country special and kept it ahead of the curve our big ideas, like the Constitution, the Bill of Rights, due process, the assembly line, the computer, the internet, the first national postal service, refrigeration, the sewing machine, the light bulb, the telephone, and so on.

Throughout our history, we have exhibited a strong propensity to think outside the box, explore new possibilities, and, if necessary, fly in the face of established convention. Our forefathers didn't establish the way of life we enjoy today by achieving, recording, or relying on aptitude scores. They did it with common sense, open minds, and profound vision. The TAKS measures none of the three.

The public and political outcry that led to the creation of the TAKS was feathered a whole lot like Chicken Little. A few parents got tired of being told their children were behind the international curve on scholastic aptitude tests, that their substandard performances would keep their children from competing in the workplace, and that this national deficiency was one of the reasons so many of our jobs were being lost to smarter folks overseas. We now know those "smarter" folks overseas were just cheaper.   It's true that kids in places like Japan score higher, on average, than our children on aptitude exams, but predictably so–Japanese culture doesn't encourage diversity, nonconformity, or independent thinking. If our kids continue to be intellectually hamstrung by the current TAKS-based curricula, in which administrators keep learning strategies strictly focused on the test-taking tunnel, we'll catch up with Japan, et al., in no time. But is that what we really want?

If we stay on top for generations to come, it will have nothing to do with the TAKS test. It will depend on the freedom and judgment we grant our educators in their efforts to educate and inspire our children. Correlating their performance on aptitude exams with their success as human beings or mandating that they standardize their talents and abilities to meet statistics instead of unique situations will simply squander our greatest natural resource.

Our children are no dumber or slower than we were. What's kept us on top all these years is imagination, fostered by diversity, inspired teaching, and independent thinking. Our hopes for the future don't rest in the hands of the docile students who excel at these tests. Our hopes for the future roil in the fertile minds of kids who are currently bored or daydreaming.

A Wealth of Murderous Stupidity

Dissident Voice • *May 15, 2007*

I read about an interesting study the other day. It said that intelligence was not linked to wealth. My response was monosyllabic.

Duhhhh.

According to a recent Ohio State University study published in the journal *Intelligence*, there is no connection between brain and earning power.

You'd think this revelation would have been self-evident. Making money usually requires work. But a large accumulation of monetary or material wealth requires stinginess, greed and a sense of entitlement more than hard work or intellectual prowess.

One's propensity for stinginess and greed has to be rooted deeply enough to override his or her more noble impulses, and one's sense of entitlement has to be so pronounced that it squelches rationality and stunts conscience. Once the wings of our better angels have been clipped, we are free to covet, grub after and hoard the spoils of Capitalism in relative peace.

It's not very ethical and it's arguably not very smart, but it's the only game around these days, right?

Wrong.

There are primitive tribes living in the Amazon basin that would probably fill you full of poison-tipped blow-darts if you told them the world was round, but they're smart enough not to base success in their societies on having more than their share, using more than they need or screwing over the folks in the wigwam next door to get ahead. They haven't been introduced to the American Way and, obviously, this makes them at least a little better and smarter than us. Especially since they live in harmony with their habitat and we're destroying ours (and theirs).

They don't have a written language. They don't know algebra. They don't live in high-rises, posh lofts or quarter-acre chunks of suburban heaven. They don't have air conditioning, hot showers or alarm clocks. And they don't have bank accounts or private property. But they know how to survive in the natural world and they have sense enough to care whether or not how they're living impacts their home.

For years we've done our industrialized best to root them out, perhaps because they are the antithesis of what we've become. We are consumers; they are conservers. We are wasting, poisoning or destroying every natural resource we utilize. They live in harmony with their habitat.

With various forms of environmental peril impending with each step of Western progress, perhaps it's time we looked to them for wisdom.

We're not smarter than them. We've just been exposed to more ideas. We mistake almost universal technological dependence for progress, rote sophistication for complexity and reading the *New York Times* or the *Wall Street Journal* at Starbucks (while sipping on a Frappuchino) for intellectual development.

We consider these primitives brutish, savage and ignorant. But they're not killing each other over fossil fuels, rotting away from dozens of stress-related ailments or searching everywhere except inward for truth, God and the meaning of life.

And speaking of God, I have it on good information that Jesus Christ was a pretty sharp primitive himself. In fact, one of the only things Christians get right these days—at least in their portrayal of Christ—is his material modesty. He'd give away anything he had. He'd share his last morsel of sustenance rather than hide it from others or hoard it for himself.

True Christianity is the antithesis of Capitalism. Capitalism is based on using one's energy, talent or cunning to acquire wealth. This was beneath Christ. It'd be nice if it were beneath us. Or at least not held up as what determines our worth.

Saying that the acquisition of wealth requires intelligence is like saying that murder requires courage.

If we can't find a kinder, gentler system of commerce or economic relations—a system that doesn't reward insatiable greed, perpetually inflated profit margins, ruthless self-interest and reckless over-consumption—then we are murderers.

Of primitives, of this planet and of our own natural integrity.

The Manipulated Mob
Fort Worth Weekly • *September 5, 2006*

Goethe used to say that whenever he heard the word "democracy," he reached for his revolver. When I was a younger idealist, I couldn't understand that. It didn't make sense.

Now that I'm older and have spent a decade or so in the real world and observed the last couple of presidential elections, I think I know what he was talking about. The problem with democracy is an uninformed electorate. The cretinous mob. The ignorant majority who by sheer force of numbers marginalizes and frequently alienates the subsequent minority of different, independent, and often enlightened individuals who inhabit the fringes of the culture. Fringe-dwellers almost inevitably suffer at the whim of the mob or majority because that mob or majority is a gullible, skittish, easily manipulated herd.

And that's what we've become. A gullible, skittish, easily manipulated herd. There may be two political parties and therefore two different trail drivers, but they're driving the same dimwitted herd. And we—the herd—are bovinely trudging down so many malevolent paths that peril and ruin seem a foregone conclusion.

Religious fundamentalists say what's happening in the Middle East is a sign of the "end times." Environmentalists are saying the ecosystem is being sabotaged so quickly that human life will be unsustainable in an evolutionary blink of the eye. Conservatives claim that the negative characterization of anything President Bush says or does is just a subversive conspiracy perpetrated by the Liberal Media. Liberals believe conservative values are at least borderline fascist and charge that conservative motives are tinged with prejudice, greed, and ruthlessness.

We are constantly barraged by a dizzying spate of calculated political grandstanding and corrosive, polarizing rhetoric. We find ourselves scurrying into any and every rabbit hole of distraction and escapism to achieve a detached complacency—and that's the closest we get to peace and happiness. Proverbially speaking, to think is to undermine, ignorance is bliss, and the meek shall inherit the earth.

The problem with ignorant bliss, detached complacency and meek heirs is that they make us accomplices. Accomplices to the greatest crimes in history, conspirators to the darkest treacheries, complicit in the end even to our own distress, downfall, and possibly avoidable demise. Better stated, then, ignorance is bleak, complacency is a dangerous trap, and the meek will not inherit the earth—they'll either render it uninhabitable or destroy it outright.

If the end is near, if catastrophes and calamities (human-made and otherwise) lie ahead, they'll come because we succumbed to the whisper campaigns of think-tank operatives or swore by the party lines of profit-serving political agents or contented ourselves with the finely spun dicta of partisan apologists like Ann Coulter or the celluloid bombast of Michael Moore. We have become the undiscerning choir of preachers, priests, professors, politicians, radio personalities, talk-show pundits, and fashionable causes celebre. We allow ourselves to be stuffed with opinions, positions, and perspectives like hapless Thanksgiving turkeys, and if destruction befalls us it will most likely be because we were too busy and/or too lazy to educate ourselves, stay informed, and think independently.

For a representative democracy to work, its constituents cannot be programmable automatons. They must be sentient and reasoning. They must be conscientious and—probably most important—curious. Every election—especially these days—is a trial. Every voter is a juror. Rendering a verdict or a vote without due process and due diligence is dangerous, dishonest, and disgraceful.

Where to start? Probably wherever you haven't been looking. Perhaps with whomever you ignore. Certainly whatever you refused to consider before.

There are no important lines to read between in the sports pages. There is no profundity in high fashion. There is no logic in blind faith. There is no objectivity in a party line. There are no ethical or moral principles in a checkbook vote. It won't be easy, and it may not be fun. But it makes you a valid participant in the democratic process.

According to 19th-century American theologian Tryon Edwards, "Hell is truth seen too late." I think many of us—even after being stuffed and obligatorily chirping along with whatever limited choruses we've been exposed to—have some sense that the times we live in are increasingly hellish.

This won't change unless we can transcend our close-mindedness, our contrariness, and our prejudices. Democracy is not a passive right. It's an active privilege. It's a responsibility.

We have been irresponsible and remiss.

We are an ignorant mob.

That's what makes us gullible, skittish, and easily manipulated. Only you and I can change this.

I'd like to say Goethe was an effete cynic with no faith in humanity. But what passes for democracy in America these days makes him look like a prophetic sage.

Trickle-Down Ignorance

Dissident Voice • November 7, 2008

A few weeks back, a seventh grader who hangs around the neighborhood told my kids that Obama was a stupid Muslim terrorist and that if that "nigger" got elected he and his family were moving to Canada.

A week ago, my ten-year-old daughter related the new joke going around her elementary school: What's the difference between Obama and Simba? Simba is an African lion and Obama is a lyin' African.

And the day after the election, in a high school lunch-line, a kid standing behind my fifteen-year-old son appeared to be sulking. A teenage girl asked him what was wrong. "There's a Nigger in the White House now," he said. "Yeah, I know," the girl replied. "I don't like him either."

As a parent of mixed-race children, I obviously find the ignorance inherent in these sentiments offensive. But I am not upset with the children who parrot them. I'm unhappy with their parents.

Teenagers are not genetically predisposed to call African Americans "niggers." That kind of prejudice starts at home. Ten-year-olds don't independently question Barrack Obama's integrity or sit up thinking of ways to mock half of his ethnicity. It's something they get from mom or dad as he or she relates a joke from work. And young middle school students don't instinctively suspect Obama is a Muslim or a terrorist; this kind of obtuseness starts at the parental level.

The "trickle-down" approach to economics may have been proven to be to a terrible blunder of late, but the moniker itself is solid. It's simply misapplied.

Wealth doesn't trickle down. Ignorance does.

If a child's parents are members of the Ku Klux Klan or the Aryan Nation or are simply active, vocal racists, chances are that child will also pursue repugnant ideologies or discriminate against ethnic minorities. If a child's father hangs out on street corners holding up signs that say "God Hates Fags," the chances of that child someday becoming a homophobic bumpkin who is afraid of gay marriage increase exponentially.

If mom and dad are shallow, xenophobic Neocons who mock anyone whom they're instructed to feel threatened by or disagree with, little Timmy is much more inclined to mock or denigrate anyone he is instructed to feel threatened by or disagree with.

To an absurd, sinister degree, racism, sexism, homophobia, prejudice, narrow-mindedness and insensitivity are passed down through too many families in this country, from the grandparents to the parents and from the parents to the kids, like precious family heirlooms.

Hence, ignorance and cruelty continually dim our collective future by trickling down from generation to generation, miring us in an unsavory wealth of malevolence and woe.

I think the American poet Anne Sexton put it best when she wrote "Live or die, but don't poison everything."

If you're so eat up with hate and fear that you can't abide the skin color or free will or liberty of others because your fascist, close-minded daddy and/or mommy or "good" book told you so, fine. But keep it to yourself.

No offense, but the world would be a better place if the chains for which you are a part of are broken. And if you'll stop stuffing your children like Thanksgiving turkeys with your paranoia and prejudices, they might grow up with minds of their own, figuring out things for themselves.

Trust me, as a fellow parent—for my kids and yours—life is too short for them to spend years trying to transcend what we've done to them.

It's worth a try, right?

Author Bio

Born in Fort Worth and raised in Aledo, writer E.R. Bills received a degree in journalism from Texas State University. He is the author of *Texas Obscurities: Stories of the Peculiar, Exceptional and Nefarious* (The History Press, 2013), *The 1910 Slocum Massacre: An Act of Genocide in East Texas* (The History Press, 2014) and *Black Holocaust: The Paris Horror and a Legacy of Texas Terror* (Eakin Press, 2015). His work has also appeared in *Fort Worth Weekly*, *Fort Worth Magazine*, the *Fort Worth Star-Telegram*, the *Austin American-Statesman* and numerous other publications.

Come and Take It (Brain)

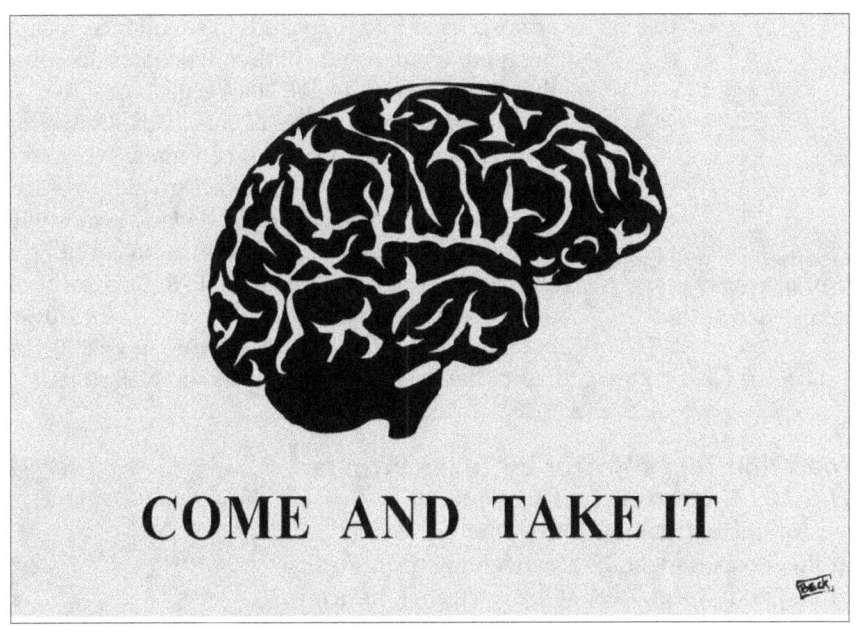

Merchandise Available at www.Zazzle.com
Search Texas Dissident

More Eakin Press Titles

Black Holocaust: The Paris Horror and a Legacy of Texas Terror
by E.R. Bills

Paperback • 198 pages
ISBN 9781681790176
Retail Price $19.95

From 1891 to 1922, Texans burned an average of one person of color at the stake a year for three decades. These burnings typically featured carnival atmospheres with thousands in attendance, including men, women and children who later described the spectacles as jovial "barbecues" or "roasts," and commemorated the events with "lynching" postcards. It was a period when many white Texans-previously enraged by Reconstruction-reasserted white primacy and terrorized black Texans with impunity. Join author E. R. Bills in this recounting of an African American holocaust. E. R. Bills is a Texas author and historian who also wrote "The 1910 Slocum Massacre: An Act of Genocide in East Texas" and "Texas Obscurities:: Stories of the Peculiar, Exceptional and Nefarious."

Road Kill: Texas Horror by Texas Writers
Edited by E.R. Bills & Bret McCormick

An ancient demon plays cowboy and takes on the Texas Rangers. Three teenage girls sneak into a "body farm." An aging African American couple defies the Grim Reaper. An FBI agent discovers an entire city that's gone to the "dogs." A handyman learns that the fixer-upper he's working on has a doorway to the past that's way out of square. And a pack of possums gets into politics. Join seventeen Texas authors for a supernatural spin on the twisting freeways and dark back roads that wind through the Lone Star State.

Texas writers that contributed to this book include David Bowles, Joe R. Lansdale, Anna L. Davis, E. R. Bills, Stephen Patrick, Carmen Gray, Bret McCormick, Russell C. Connor, Michael H. Price, Tom Bont, Ernie Lee, David Robledo, Alan Beauvais, Michael Baldwin, Glen Coburn, Joe McKinney and Tom Alexander.

Paperback • 238 pages
ISBN 9781681790794
Retail Price • $16.95